UN-ADOPTABLE?

Faith Beyond Foster Care

Janelle Molony

The stories and conversations in this book are based on true events but are altered to conceal non-essential or private information to the best of the author's ability. In addition, no information or opinions in this book should be considered a substitute for the advice, decisions, or judgement of a qualified medical or mental health professional. The author expressly disclaims responsibility for any adverse effects arising from the use or application of the information shared within.

Cover design by 99Designs.com/Klassic Designs
Cover image by Unsplash/Anna Kolosyuk @anko_
Book layout by Ekow Addai
Author headshot by Dana Kirkland

Print (Hardback): 978-1-7344638-0-4 ($19.95)
Print (Paperback): 978-1-7344638-1-1 ($16.95)
EBook: 978-1-7344638-2-8 ($9.95)

Faith-based family and parenting memoir.
Genre: Parenting / Family
Web: JanelleMolony.com and AdoptionToLife.com

UN-ADOPTABLE?

Faith

BEYOND FOSTER CARE

Dedication

To my Grandparents, Ralph and Marie.

They fostered children in the 1950s, loving every single child in their care. When they spoke of the blind boy, or the half-Japanese girl, and finally being able to adopt their first son, their emotions poured out to fill the room like the scent of a sweet, holiday pie. Sharing with Grandma my plan to start a family through adoption was one of our last conversations. Later, I'd tell my grandfather I wrote a book all about it before he also passed on. They are both deeply missed.

Contents

Praise For *Un-Adoptable?*

"A candid and courageous account of a loving, deeply committed first and later adoptive Mom who not only survived being put to the test, but triumphed. A must-read for anyone contemplating fostering or adopting a child. In short, a sobering heads up! As a psychologist, I was truly awed by the accounts of "David's' age regressions. Janelle describes it in such detail, and with such psychological insight, that she could teach a class in child psychopathology. Talk about being put to the test. I'll bet some prospective foster and adoption folks would read that and have a sobering reckoning: 'If I'm honest with myself, am I made of the stuff that made it possible for Janelle and Ryan to persevere?'"

Dr. P. Leslie Herold, Professor of Psychology, Cal-State. Co-Creator of the award-winning *Co-Parenting Training Program at Solutions for Families.*

"Janelle shares her journey of navigating the (foster care) system and fighting to create a family with a stranger. My favorite part is when she explains how childrens' profiles are interpreted. This book is going to be helpful for foster and adoptive parents, those working in behavioral health, and almost anyone with an interest in family development. Janelle tells readers to: 1. Do their research, 2. Have a strong support system, and 3. Don't feel ashamed if things go south."

Morgan Comeau, Community-Based Family Support

"I'm not a behavioralist or a psychologist or psychiatrist. I am just a mom… a mom who loves and refuses to give up (on my child). Everything Janelle said is true and I most certainly "get it." I've wanted to share our story for so long and wished to be able to tell others what happens. In her story, Janelle does."

Teri-Lynn Manning, Adoptive Parent

There is something in her writing that knits "us" together. There are just things other people can't relate to. But Janelle can and does. Everything is spot on.

Kacee Cruz, Adoptive Parent

"This was a nice read and it left me wanting to read more. It kept my interest and felt real, kind, raw and honest. It'll be a story that will resonate and interest people who can relate to this journey in a big, big way. Janelle's connection to people with special needs children and those with foster/adoption stories is fabulous. Her blog (AdoptionToLife.com) has also been truly transformative for me and my family. Janelle knows how to speak to and IMPACT families for the better!! I believe her style of writing and the way she strings a story together is compelling and offers a ton of readability. Thanks for sharing!"

Debbie Gill Cross, Special Needs Parent

"It's a very moving book. It makes me want to read more and find out what eventually happened to the little boy."

Cheri Basset, Occupational Therapist, Pillar Child Development

Foreword

Lesia Knudsen

Un-Adoptable? Faith Beyond Foster Care, is beautifully written, amazingly accurate, and inspiring.

In the memoir, Janelle Molony shines a spotlight on the reality and heartaches that often come with foster parenting and adoption. The painful, yet miraculous story will leave you full of hope, joy, empathy, and compassion.

Her honesty and transparency gives prospective and current parents the courage to feel things we think we're not supposed to feel, but do on a regular basis. Her story gives us permission to feel like a failure, make mistakes, or feel like quitting, without condemnation or guilt. Then, she bolsters the reader with hope for the future.

As a foster parent myself, I continuously tend to the heartache and pain of the children we care for. Janelle captured the raw and unfiltered emotions we regularly experience as we watch the children struggle with the reality of their situations.

By sharing her story, frees readers to say, "Hey, I felt that, too. But I'm still a good mom/dad, and it's going to be okay."

This book is a must-read for everyone who is currently providing care or considering foster care or adoption. In addition, social workers, therapists, church officials, and medical practitioners will benefit from seeing their impact on our families.

By reading this book, you will gain knowledge, wisdom, and compassion for the little ones; seeing the heart of God for the orphan demonstrated through the pouring out of truly unconditional love.

Un-Adoptable? is a story of God's healing and transformative power demonstrated a family who said, "Yes!" to God and, "Yes!" to committing to a little boy they were told was "unadoptable," yet now, is destined for great things.

Lesia Knudsen

Parent Coach, Marin County Child and Family Services, California

Author of *Life in the Foster Lane, Practical Insights on Fostering Teens*

International speaker and foster parenting advocate

LesiaKnudsen.com

Introduction

"*What am I supposed* to call you?" The little boy from the backseat asked. We had just picked him up from a Child Protective Services office to take him out for lunch and to play video games at the mall. We didn't know the protocol for this. We just met last week—once.

"You can call us whatever you want."

He knew his answer. "I want to call you Mom and Dad."

The drive back to the office was tense. My husband, Ryan, and I held a silent eye-conversation with each other that I believe sounded like, "Um, that's cool. Is this okay? I like it, do you? Yeah, I'm okay with it. It's kind of weird though. And fast. Yeah.

Really fast."

Ryan and I had been on the waiting list for a foster child over a year. The only other time we had heard about a child we could meet was at Christmas, six months prior. He was a two-year-old boy. We said yes.

I wrapped some presents for him and tucked them under the tree. I had all his clothes in the dresser and decorated the nursery with the cutest monkey theme. We knew the transfer process from this baby's foster home to ours would begin within five days. Anticipation was high in our hearts, and our church community had surrounded us with prayers and support such as hand-me-down clothes.

But this soon-to-be family was terminated before it could ever start. A biological grandparent stepped up and took the child in.

"How could they?" I was pissed and heartbroken. *Selfish, for sure.*

Last-Minute Marmie gets to be a mom (again). And I now have to swallow the biggest rejection pill ever. Everywhere I go, I'd be showing up "childless," and everyone in my community would wonder what happened.

Adoption isn't for the faint of heart. It's hard.

Adopting from foster care is a special kind of hard.

This is my story. It is not everyone's story, but I feel like it resonates with many families who have been or will be on this path. I didn't write it to give anyone instructions. It's not meant to scare or upset people. But I hope that you do find direction and guard your heart. When you open yourself to a child who has experienced trauma, such as many foster youths have, your life will take on a direction of its own.

So, how did this start? Well, shortly after I married my best friend, Ryan, we were having those long conversations about the future. Children came up. Without going into detail, it was likely I could get pregnant, but not-so-likely I could sustain a pregnancy. This wasn't sad news. More like, "Oh. Huh." We weren't planning on having kids right away, so it would be easy to set this matter aside for a decade.

Then, on a long walk around the park one day, I wondered aloud, "What if we just adopted?"

He said, "That's okay. I would love any child we got as if they were my own." And that's where the conversation stopped—for five years.

I never had any strong urges to be a mother in this time. My girlfriends told me about the day when my "baby clock" would tick. I brushed it off.

Then one day it hit me.

"Let's adopt."

Just like that. No, not, "Let's have a baby..." but a very simple, "It's time. Let's adopt."

It was from there we began an agency search. This became my project, somehow. Some call it a "paper pregnancy." Completing paperwork and making phone calls was irritating, but my handwriting was more legible than Ryan's and I had more patience for this kind of stuff. So, I sat through open houses and orientations alone at first, vetting several agencies that dealt with private, foster, minority, religious, LGBT, and you-name-it adoptions. Now, let me warn you—each agency has an agenda. They are in their niche for a reason. And there were pros and cons to each.

Money was always a huge factor. Those who could pay $30,000 cash would get infants. Those who couldn't should expect a child over the age of seven. We fell into the latter category. Mostly because we were broke. But also because we didn't want to buy a baby. That seemed wrong to us. We didn't need an infant *that* bad.

I finally selected a semi-religious, semi-local, and semi-minority based agency. This happened by way of orientation follow-up calls.

Without naming names, there were some racists in my family (this is not a joke). So, it was important to find an agency that would help us navigate the system in a way that we would not be bringing a child into a situation which would be unwelcoming. It didn't seem responsible or fair.

"So, um, I just need to know if our family situation would be a problem?" I asked the representative of an agency. I remember receiving a personally written letter responding to my call. It said that our application was now closed.

Great. My racist family had already screwed this up and we had barely even begun!

A few more agency calls later, I finally talked to an amazing woman named Carol. She reassured me we would have many opportunities to see and search through all the childrens' profiles to find a good fit. Sold!

As it turned out, the agency was two hours away from us, so I committed Ryan and myself to an immense trek for training every weekend for two months. The six-hour sessions included learning how the foster system worked, how to set up and manage our home, and how trauma and attachment impact the brain. Let me just say, that *wasn't* enough.

Looking back, there should have been more about what happens with the day-to-day logistical drama when the child is living with you. And then there should have been a session on what to expect before the adoption (so many extra surprises). And most importantly, there should have been training on preparing your heart for the long-haul after adoption that is now your actual "life."

Unlike a marriage, adoption is nearly irreversible. To rescind or "dissolve" an adoption is (in some states) a misdemeanor crime of child abuse. Adopting a child from foster care was the most serious commitment I have ever made in my life.

The Christmas sermon at church was on how God loved the world so much that he gave his Son as a gift to the world in order to redeem us from our sinful lives. The pastor was good with rhetorical speech. Normally, I would have appreciated it, but that last year was different.

"Alright church, how would YOU finish this sentence," he offered. "'If God really loved me *that much*, he would...?'"

"He'd give me a child!"

My memory is not perfect, but I might have yelled that aloud.

"How'd it go?" Upon returning to the Child Protective Services office, the little boy's social worker asked about our play date. He was taken away into another room, to be rejoined with his current foster family. This conversation allowed our adoption agency worker to study us. It felt like a test. After many match failures, application rejections, and agency interceptions... how did we do with our first successful match?

This day, we observed that the little boy was desperately hungry, had no sense of stranger danger, was noticeably uncoordinated, and carried a spirit of sadness over his head. Something was odd. But, according to the social worker's report, he had no medical concerns. This was a key reason for the match.

Remember this detail.

I don't remember what we said exactly, but I know we asked them about the boy wanting to call us "Mom" and "Dad," during the visit. Now it was the agency worker and social worker's turn to have an eye-conversation.

What weren't they telling us?

Chapter 1

Help! I Don't Speak "Foster"

"*Sihara and Jacob. Siblings.* Five and two. Sihara is in Kindergarten. She likes art and horses. She has an IEP."[1] I was reading a child's profile to my husband.

"Aww... she is cute! Look at her with her little, stuffed pony." We stopped to stare at her picture and make a thousand guesses as to what she acted like, sounded like, if her hair was soft, or if she would like our dog. In these cases, the pictures were *not* worth more than the words, however.

The stories provided were brief, cryptic code-talk about the children in the foster system. The kids we saw were at a point in their

1 An IEP is an Individualized Education Plan. This document includes the results of academic and psychological testing, classroom evaluations, and medical reports for the student. It identifies specific disabilities or disadvantages that require accommodations in a classroom.

case when they needed to be placed long-term or adopted. Most of the biological parents were either disqualified to reunify with their children (per certain criminal statutes) or would soon have their parental rights terminated.

While *we* were looking over their pictures and trying to imagine a life with them, *their* family was being legally disembodied. This included their current foster home, which would not be moving forward towards adoption. All the children we looked at would soon go through an upheaval.

"Jacob is learning to crawl. He is very curious. He was exposed in utero but has been making steady progress. He loves to smile," I read further. His picture showed him on his belly looking up and smiling with his eyes closed. I had to wonder, if this was supposed to be a photo of him in his best light, why wasn't he posed differently, or the photo retaken with his eyes open? Who took these photos, anyway?

The last section read, "TPR[2] hearing set. Weekly visitations with a biological grandparent. Parents will need to be patient and encouraging. The siblings may be placed together or individually."

My gut sank. We were quickly learning to read between the lines when reviewing these profiles. Each time we received a profile, we would e-mail in a response form stating our interest level, what we felt like matched with our search criteria, and what we would need more clarity on. Then, our agency would compare this child's

---

2 The hearing is referred to as either the "TPR" (Termination of Parental Rights), or the .26 / "two-six hearing," because it is referring to the Welfare and Institutions Code (WIC) §366.26. It is at this hearing that a "permanency plan" is set in motion, whether it means a return to biological family or another care plan such as guardianship or adoption.

situation with our family profile and either submit our home study record to the child's social worker to move forward, or send a reply e-mail saying:

> *"Thank you for considering these children. We have some concerns that will prevent us from moving forward with a match. Please re-read the profile. Call us with any questions."*

I called this an interception.

The agency acted like they knew better than us as to which kids would be a good fit for our family. Even though we said we would be fine with children having certain features or disabilities, *they* disagreed. This was irking, at best. I thought, as the parents, we would have more of the final say. As it turned out, we did. We just had little to no *initial* say.

After a short call with the agency, our eyes would be opened to what the profiles were and were not disclosing. For example, if Sihara's were more honest, it would say the following:

> *Sihara is in Kindergarten. She isn't cooperative with teachers. She won't play with the other kids. She struggles with reading and math. She has an Individualized Educational Program (IEP) because of some incidents at the school. She receives group social skills classes and special education services. She prefers to draw pictures, rather than use her words. She goes to horse therapy every weekend to assist with anger management.*

With trained eyes, she sounded like a bomb about to blow.

Now let's look at Jacob:

> *Jacob is severely delayed. He is two and cannot yet crawl. He may end up being wheelchair bound if he can't learn to become mobile. He is also, likely, still in diapers. He touches everything with an unexpected intensity. He is highly sensitive to physical sensory inputs. This is how he experiences and navigates his world. He was exposed in-utero, but we aren't going to tell you the substances involved. That's confidential.*
>
> *Improvements have been noted with responding positively to sound, including voices. Jacob is transitioning from an all-liquid to a semi-solid diet. He doesn't quite make eye contact but likes to turn his face toward the warm sunlight. No official medical diagnosis has been made at this point.*

Poor baby! This is the kind of thing that breaks down a parent who *isn't* on drugs. Caring for a child with fetal alcohol syndrome or other brain-altering disorders requires an emotional fortitude Ryan and I were not certain we had.

We would also *not* conjure it. Our agency coached us towards finding a family member, not a "project." I realize that word isn't kind, but this is actually what the agency used.

"Remember, you guys are looking to build your family, not take on a project." Then they went on to explain how some people specifically take on more difficult cases. These special people are of the mindset that this is part of their mission or responsibility to the world. Or, they may have special qualifications such as a medical background. Or, they are in this for the money.

Caretakers for children with greater medical needs typically receive a higher monthly stipend from the state. The funds are intended to cover the expenses incurred by the child. By "higher," this could mean upwards to, or more than $20,000 per year—untaxed.

The money sounds nice, but it comes with a cost to the child and family. Hard-to-raise children are exactly that: hard to raise. Seeds of love do not readily grow on hardened soil. Every penny (and more) could be funneled into extensive treatments, if the desired outcome was a loving relationship. People who get into foster care for the wrong reasons aren't fostering emotional connections, promoting healing, or hoping for love in the relationship. Or eye contact.

We wanted more. Advice: taken.

As such, we would fill out our response form with a "no." *That sucked.* Doing this made me feel selfish, ugly, and like a bad mom already. This guilt was something akin to pushing a huge, red "reject" button that would send the children down a metal slide into foster care purgatory. And they would know that I pushed it.

A voice in my head spoke. "Think of it this way: If someone gave you a choice to have a healthy or disabled child, which would you choose?" Healthy, of course. That's every parent's dream. It was an easy answer when posed hypothetically.

"So make that choice," the voice concluded.

It sounded so simple. And logical.

I think this voice belonged to Misty. She was a hippie lady with a thick streak of grey running through her bangs. Misty was the social worker assigned to our family for post-placement care. She worked for the adoption agency and her goal was to help us make it through the ups and downs we would face and *stay* a family. She was an angel. I truly felt she wanted us to succeed and be happy.

If the last section of Sihara and Jacob's profile had been more honest, it might have sounded like this:

> *Their parents have been given their prescribed number of chances to get the children back. They have either fulfilled their requirements or failed. Now, parental rights will either be granted back to them, or severed at the .26 hearing. The judge will decide if there will be a termination of parental rights (TPR) and the children released to be adopted by someone else.*
>
> *In addition to having these children in your life, you will also coordinate time for a grandparent to visit them. The grandparent has continued to show love and support, but cannot adopt the children. It is undecided at this time if the courts will request that the adoption remains open to ongoing contact. Parents will need to be patient and encouraging because healthy connections to the biological family are instrumental in being able to make new connections in the attachment process.*
>
> *Finally, we understand one child may have a greater demand for care than the other. We also know these children are young enough to overcome a separation. Depending on your family plans, you can apply for one or both. But hurry, because the one with lesser needs will likely go fast.*

What would you do? Would you separate them?

This concept of splitting siblings was hard for me to fathom. It felt so, very wrong. *Who would do that?* I suppose I could understand if there were five or more kids and that was too much for one family to take in at once. But to split these precious babies apart from their *only* sibling? I couldn't. We wouldn't.

But this is exactly what would happen to our son.

We had to make a choice. Of the eight profiles we received in this month's available match listings, these siblings were the only ones that came close to what we were looking for. By saying "no," that would be the end of this month's search. Disappointment and loneliness ate at me.

We turned them both down.

"Maybe we'll find the right 'someone' next month..." we reasoned.

Remembering why you began this journey will help you stay *on* your path. This doesn't mean the path will be straight or easy. But being *absolutely* sure about what you say "yes" and "no" to before you begin will help you avoid pitfalls and hardship.

We wanted a "forever family." A family that would last. A family with love.

We had to choose carefully. And wait.

"To thine own self, be true." - **William Shakespeare.**

When we first began this journey, we did not realize how carefully *we* would be screened as the foster-adoptive parents. Before being matched with a child, we needed to complete an in-depth background check and interview referred to as the "home study." The home study process involved the same scrutiny and caution we were taught to apply when looking at potential family additions. After all, a healthy, long-term relationship *should* be established with care.

Our adoption agency wanted to know who we were and how we came to be in the position to start a family through adoption. This involved digging into our pasts and taking no risky chances with our futures.

After a thorough examination of our medical records, driver records, job histories, criminal backgrounds, bank records, social media accounts, and personal reference letters, Mr. Wells, the agency director, had a starting point for our interview.

"I see here, you have a history of alcohol abuse," Mr. Wells eyed my husband after flipping through our documents. Uh-oh. Here we go.

Honesty is truly *the* best policy when it comes to completing your home study. Ryan used to be a different type of person before we married. I had met him in the first year of his sobriety. I never met the person others had known. His own sister, who had introduced us, said to me once, "He used to drink…" as if that explained everything.

It didn't. That was her way of hinting without telling. Just like the child profiles do.

The theory behind this specific inquiry was that my husband would have a higher likelihood to repeat his prior behaviors, should he not maintain his sobriety. This factor would be considered a very real risk to any child placed in our home. If this happened, my husband could potentially trigger the child or add to their trauma. We did not like this presumption at all.

"I never liked that guy," Ryan told me recently. "He always seemed to have it out for me." I agree with those sentiments. Mr. Wells never really seemed to believe Ryan was serious about or ready for fathering a child.

Included in our documentation, I'd photocopied over six years of sobriety "chips" that Ryan had collected in his support group. Mr. Wells never mentioned this fact in the interview.

Now, I could see the same reading-between-the-lines strategy that the agency used with childrens' profiles was being used on us. In the interviewing process, Mr. Wells left no stone unturned.

My turn. "And you have been on anti-depressants?" he asked, lowering his reading glasses to consider me. Why was it that this guy used the same reproachful tone of voice for these two very different histories?

"Yes," I said defensively. "I had anxiety in college. A long time ago." Lots of people do. Where was he going with this? It was uncomfortable.

Here is my unconfirmed hypothesis on the inquisition: The agency would ultimately use this information against us in the match process. Perhaps "against" is too strong of a word? No, it isn't. Be forewarned.

I understand that safety for the children is of the utmost importance. If anything we revealed in the home study could be considered a predictor of future behaviors, then it is the duty of the social workers to note it in our profile. Unfortunately, this same level of prudence wouldn't be applied when we were being introduced to our future son.

Our histories would translate like this:

> *Ryan has an increased likelihood of relapse. Do not place children with prior exposure to alcohol abuse under his care.*
>
> *Janelle does not do well under stress. Do not place children with high needs under her care.*

As it turned out, we received a child with prior exposure *and* high needs. I realized later that the agency had the best of intentions to avoid this situation. Perhaps I should not have taken so much offense to their cross-examination.

One day, I poured a glass of wine for myself. After all, mom's got to have some wine sometimes—especially with such a "stressful" child placement. The tiny little boy had been in our home for a very short time.

The boy tagged along a short distance behind me into the kitchen. He did this often. He never wanted to be farther than five feet from me. He even sat inside the bathroom while I *went* to the bathroom. *Turn around, kid.* If I tried to close the door, he would go into an explosive panic. I don't know how to explain this other than there being an on/off switch in his head.

If a door (or wall) separated us, he'd instantaneously burst into tears, scream, and claw at or pound on the offending divider.

"Mommy, don't go!" He *lost* it.

"Please, Mommy, let me in! Can I come in....? I'll be good, I promise!" The dramatics hinted at some deeper issues we had yet to be informed of. *Yikes.*

I just need a few minutes alone. Please.

In the kitchen, he watched what I was doing with the glass. *On.*

He panicked. "Noooo!"

A blur of flailing olive-tone limbs, he ran a full circle around the kitchen, bumped into a cupboard, and fell to the ground crying, "I don't want a drunk mommy!!"

Again?

The puddle was writhing and pulling on his face. He was experiencing very real pain; reliving something so scary that he'd have to wrestle a demon in order to come to. What did I do? What *do* I do?

Irritated, confused and taken aback, I felt helpless. It wasn't Ryan they needed to worry about. It was me. This child was now scared of me. The guilt and shock I felt were heavy. Honestly, I felt like a piece of trash.

At this time, I could not separate *my* relationship to the boy from *his* relationship with his biological mother. I thought he hated and feared everything about me. Eventually, this would lead me down the dark path of depression.

It would take a good, long time for us to desensitize him and this type of reaction. And desensitize him, I would, because I liked closing my bedroom door, bathroom door... and Merlot.

Part of this involved allowing the boy to see the bottle of wine sit, and sit, and sit. Out on the counter. Untouched. Rarely opened.

This broke a major foster care rule. Alcohol is supposed to be locked up. But I somehow understood what he needed to see and to *feel* in order to gain a sense of peace on this matter. We could always lock it up on the social worker's visiting days, as needed.

Breaking this rule would result in a stern warning from the social workers and a note added to our file regarding non-compliance. Immediate proof of corrective action would be sought (and possibly required retraining on the rules). If these types of behaviors continued unaddressed, our foster care license could be revoked. I had to be careful.

I also made this boy a promise to never, ever be a "drunk mommy." To this very day, I have kept this commitment to him.

Chapter 2

There Is No Such Thing As a Perfect Match

"*We found a boy,*" the caller said. I was driving when the phone rang.

Ohmygosh. I don't know where I was, but I remember pulling the car over to take this call. It was important. Every single call from the agency was important right now.

"Wait. Can you wait? Can I three-way Ryan into this call?" He should hear this firsthand. I got off the phone and immediately texted a bunch of 9-1-1 messages for him to stop whatever he was doing at work and CALL ME NOW. With Ryan on the phone, we brought Mr. Wells back onto the call.

"As I was saying, there is a boy we've heard about. We don't have much information on him yet. There is no profile circulating. It's sort of... being passed along by a friend." This is agency-speak for "insider trading."

The private agency we worked with navigated a handful of regional divisions to place foster youth with potential adoptive families. This meant not being limited to adopting children from only within our county. We had access to a wider pool. And, apparently, insider trading. *Pro.*

If a county received a child, they had a certain obligation to peruse the home studies of families which were local. This would make it easy to transport the child to parental visits, keep them in their local school, and with the same medical providers, etc. So, the local foster homes get first priority to receive incoming children. *Con—for us.*

In the situation where the child's parental rights are being terminated and no visitations are ordered, however, the originating county has the ability to transfer the child out to a different county. With access to additional home studies, the local social worker can more easily find a suitable long-term placement.

Our agency worked as a liaison. Or a matchmaker. They visited with different Child Welfare offices and built connections with the social workers. The social workers would share information on potentially adoptable children and our agency could get a firsthand opportunity to say something like, "I've got the perfect family for that kid." *Pro.*

Then, our home study got passed directly to the person behind the scenes, and ultimately, was added to a stack of twenty others sitting on their desk. *Con—bureaucracy was still in force.*

One time, we were in the running for a match. They had two families that would go in for the initial disclosure meeting where you learn more about the child, ask questions, and then make another yes or no decision. The social worker scheduled the *other* family's meeting before ours. ...And then we never had our meeting. The other family said yes, and that was that. We didn't even have a chance because we were second on her list, instead of first.

The lesson we learned was to always answer the phone first. Schedule first. Be there first. Almost to the point of "Act now, think about it later." These aren't words of advice. This type of aggression should be limited to a child you can fully commit to based on the barest minimum of information. I sincerely hope that *your* "barest minimum" is nothing like ours was.

"Can you tell us about him?" I prompted nervously. *Don't sound desperate.* I mentally coached myself. *Relax.*

There was a pause, then, "We think he is five. He has siblings, but they've already been adopted. He's cute and he's Caucasian. No parents are in the picture."

Okay, thanks. Except that felt like a warm-up. Even the profiles had more detail than that. And that's a *generous* use of the word "more."

"What else? Any issues?" We pressed Mr. Wells for more.

"No, we have some records, but it's all pretty clear. Allergies. Possible ADHD. Otherwise, there are no major medical concerns," he reported.

Well, dang. This sounded like an open-and-shut case! My heart was already skipping beats.

"*Will* there be a profile? Can we see a picture?" No, and no.

He clarified, "More information can be reviewed at the disclosure meeting. Do you want me to send in your home study to set it up?"

Of course, we said yes. Yes—to a vague description of a healthy child that only existed in foster fairy tales. And so, we were one step closer to our serendipitous placement.

Through a series of unbelievable events, Steven, our little boy, was at home with us. It had only been seven days, but we were growing simultaneously in fondness and trepidation. It was a honeymoon of sorts.

Then the doorbell rang. *Ack!* Protective Services was back. It was too soon! They weren't supposed to come pick him up for a few more hours.

After our afternoon play date, we decided to move forward with this seven, *not five-year-old*, boy. How the agency could have had this very basic fact wrong still bothers me. I understand that the foster system is overloaded and often social workers have too many children to keep track of. Still, a simple fact-check would have been nice.

By "move forward," we expected to begin a measured dating process. We may have had an all-day outing, followed by a sleepover the next weekend, and so on in greater quantities and frequency. Each event would prime us toward a long-term connection. It also gave us an opportunity to make an immediate 180° on our decision with the least added trauma to the child, should something arise. We were comfortable with this process.

So, he came to us for a sleepover. But for some totally understandable reason, the prior foster family couldn't pick him up the next day. He'd have to stay for the weekend. We didn't mind. It would be a busy weekend with a little stranger in tow, but it was exciting!

He came with a little child's backpack. Three outfits. Pajamas. One blankie.

Ryan and I jumped on this adventure. We took him to see the ocean for the first time. We drove him all around for sightseeing. He was shy, giggly, bouncing off the walls... never sleeping… and never bathing. And never going to the bathroom. Except in his pants. He ate anything he could reach that was edible: crackers, fruit, cheese, and plain toast. And he *begged* us for his favorite food: ten-for-a-dollar Ramen noodles. Dry pantry food was his primary target. It was a fun weekend. Nothing was too serious, yet.

And then we tried to contact the prior foster family to arrange for a meetup and child switch. No response. We tried again... no response. Since it was a weekend, we had no access to the assigned social workers who could address this. There was nothing our adoption agency could do, either. As it was, we kept this boy another night, but it didn't sit right with me. I thought we would get in trouble over this decision.

Monday came along.

"So, um, we had a nice weekend, but uhh… we still have him," I explained to one of the child's social workers, Shane. I didn't know what the protocol was. This was becoming increasingly awkward.

That current week, Ryan's father would be in town. In fact, we were expecting him anytime. We knew he was an unvetted adult. No background check could be done on him before he was around this child. This is another "no-no" in the foster world. I mentioned this to Shane.

"Let me see what I can find out," he said and ended the call. Under the circumstances, they would make an exception to this practice. It seemed like the rules were more like "guidelines," at this point. *Odd.*

Some time later, Shane called back.

"So, what we've learned is that they aren't coming back," he said. Again, I had to mull over the meaning of the words to myself, slowly. They… the *other* foster family… Can they even do that?

"What?" I blurted. "What does that mean? Like, what do we do with the kid?" We had not planned on this. There was no chance for us to prepare for what happened next.

"Can you keep him until we learn more?" Shane implored. Well, yeah. Sure. What *else* were we supposed to do?

After a quick phone call to Grandpa Improviso informing him of the extra visitor, we set to unpacking boxes of clothes and toys I had collected, and reassembled the child's room to be less for a two-year-old, and more for a seven-year-old. Goodbye monkeys.

That first week was a blast going swimming and exploring the big city while Ryan worked downtown. Grandpa's delightfully distracting presence helped this boy to mask *many* of his less desirable qualities. Ryan's dad assumed nothing, asked nothing, and just loved on the little boy. Just like that. We had no answers to any questions he may have asked, anyway.

More days went by.

The phone rang. Up until this moment, we had no idea what was happening with the boy's files, the transfer process, and such. We had no paperwork for this boy at all. No court documents said we were his caretakers. No insurance card was provided, should there be a medical issue (and there was). We had no permission to give him allergy meds nor Pepto-Bismol for his self-inflicted constipation-diarrhea cycles. Our hands were legally tied.

We were essentially strangers, or unintentional kidnappers; you choose.

Shane explained over the phone, "So, they haven't followed through with our instructions. But, per the court order, the boy must go back home. It's important for him to find closure and say goodbye to the other kids." He went on to suggest that something was suspicious about this and out of the best interests of the child, *we* should be prepared to have the boy returned to us long-term, immediately, after that foster family wraps up whatever they needed to do.

This wasn't what we signed up for. We didn't mind taking him in, but there were a lot of questions arising. For the time being, we'd be Steven's new full-time foster parents. We were not considered an adoptive placement. This was just a temporary thing.

Now might be a good time to add in the fact that the prior foster home was actually the home of Steven's extended family members. That's right—actual relatives were abandoning him! They had calculated this move.

Something clicked for me. His siblings were adopted, Mr. Wells had said. Steven was not. Red flags were going up. Family was separating family. And yes, the thought crossed my mind: Were we getting the "Sihara" or the "Jacob?"

Friday came along and we had a chat with the little boy about how he would go back to his family for a short visit. He would need to spend lots of time with the "other kids," whom we now knew to be his siblings. He would need to tell them he'd be safe in his new home and he could show them the pictures from a little album we'd made. Then, in three sleeps, we would be there to pick him up.

What we didn't say is that he would never see his siblings again. We didn't know that detail, yet.

This is now on my list of "worst" days, ever. The social workers were supposed to arrive at 2:00 p.m. Ryan was coming home early from work to make sure he could say goodbye to Steven. We were planning to eat lunch together as a family.

The boy's little backpack was all ready to go in the foyer. I snuck a small card into the front pocket. I jotted something in big letters because he couldn't read well. So, I drew some hearts, too.

"*Love, Mom and Dad.*"

We were just waiting for Ryan to come home.

Then the social workers showed up—two hours early.

The little boy shrank in a panic. Shane and some other social worker we had never met calmly took his things and waited expectantly in the foyer... as if to say, "Ma'am, we need to take him home now. Please say goodbye." It was a bit curt.

But Ryan wasn't home, yet! I tried calling. No answer. What do I do, now?

"Don't cry, don't cry, don't cry..." I was thinking of anything to stall them. At least for long enough to get Ryan on the phone. I sent a final telepathic signal, "*Ryan, Call me back! Hurry, please!*"

I hugged the shell-shocked boy who had plastered himself to the living room wall like he wanted to be swallowed up inside of the paint. I rattled off the essentials like any mom would: I would see him again soon, be good, three sleeps, etc. Don't cry.

He looked stoic, steeled and cold. He didn't cry.

Then, there was nothing else I could do.

Out the door they went.

Now I was the shell-shocked one. I just released him to an unloving home. Those people specifically did not want him. And Ryan never got to say goodbye.

"*Oh, Honey. I'm so sorry,*" I sent out. To whom? I wasn't sure.

My phone rang again. It wasn't Ryan.

Shane said, "I have a very sad boy in the backseat who would really like to talk to you." He handed the phone to a hyperventilating child, wailing in the background.

He finally broke.

"Mommy?" Steven cried.

I cried. I broke, too.

"Yes, Baby?" The mournful howl that followed said everything.

In-between his breaths, I reassured him. "Baby, Mommy loves you. And I miss you. It'll be alright. I'll see you again soon, don't worry. Go and do what you need to do. We'll be right here waiting for you."

What was happening to me? I *just* met this kid. I had no reason to feel the way I did. It was confusing and not at all what I was expecting.

Chapter 3

How Much Unravelling Could We Stomach?

Thank goodness Grandpa was there that first week! He nursed our broken hearts. Otherwise, we might have stopped eating from sadness.

In one week, Grandpa had witnessed his only son fall in love with a concerningly skinny, tan-skinned boy with legs as crooked as his teeth. Then, Grandpa would watch Ryan crumble when he arrived from work to a childless house.

"Where's Steven?" He asked.

"I tried to make them wait…" I mumbled through my frown.

In that first week, we all saw this little boy do everything he could possibly do to *not* unravel in our home. It was something like having a 45-lb Mexican jumping bean around.

Grandpa patiently waded into the baby pool with Steven as he crawled around, terrified to put his face in the water. Baths were scary for Steven, too. Grandpa read stories over and over and with funny voices. It was endearing to us all. And his being there allowed me to take some breaks. This kid was a non-stop handful! Welcome to the world of Attention-Deficit-Hyperactivity Disorder.

Then there was "the farting game."

Steven was so scared to use the toilet, he ended up with a condition called encopresis. This is a fancy word for hold-it-all-in-until-you-soil-yourself. His stomach hurt constantly. *No crap* (pun intended). Later, he ended up asking us for diapers because of this. Diapers on a seven-year-old? Oh, yes.

One way we tried to make him comfortable for his extended stay was to pass gas as openly as possible …like we were *all* seven-year-old boys.

"I have an announcement!" (*FART.*)

"Honey, could you come help me with this?" (*LONG FART.*)

He thought we were the funniest people, ever. But Grandpa... he was the "Le Pétomane" of our circus.[3] With Grandpa's help, this boy let some of his guards down, and his gas out. *Phew!* Thanks, Grandpa. This was the first of many medical conditions we would overcome with out-of-the-box thinking.

Over time, we would learn that this type of acceptance and some unconventional parenting would become the pièce de résistance that ensured our survival throughout the next few years.

3 This self-proclaimed "Fartist" could toot a tune on command at the famous Parisian Moulin Rouge.

Acceptance didn't come easily. The day we met Steven, my husband claimed he experienced a love-at-first-sight experience. I didn't.

"That's him," Ryan said.

We were in the lobby of a state run office we'd never been to before —another two hours away. An adoption agency representative was nowhere to be found. So, we signed in and sat.

Looking around the waiting room full of people, I tried not to be judgmental. There was a young girl with four children around her, and one more on the way. Men with hollow faces were being called into the back, alone. There were people with folders with more pages inside than they had teeth in their mouth. This was family services. *Yikes.* This is where, we would later find out, our future son had spent nights on the floor when a foster home transferred him *out* before the social worker had time to line up another place for him to live.

"I didn't have a home," he told me. "I had to wait for one." It disgusted me in more than one way. How does that kind of thing even happen?

It smelled bad in there.

So, we were the young, happy-to-be-there White couple, amid a rather motley crew. While I was looking at the adults, Ryan was looking at the kids. More people came and went. Then another family walked in.

Ryan leaned over to whisper to me. He nodded towards a little boy with dark hair and dark eyes. Latino? Bi-Racial? I didn't know. Clearly, he was not the Caucasian we were here to meet.

"No, Honey. That's not him."

I feel it's important to add that we *had*, in fact, applied for children of color and with many ages and abilities/disabilities. I do not harbor the same opinions as my extended family. My reaction here was truly a dismissal based on the description we received over the phone. Again, we'd *never* seen a photo of him and the physical description included an approximate age and a different ethnicity.

"He's cute," they had said. *That part was correct.*

The boy joined the other kids crawling around on the floor.

"God, this is awkward," I thought. This was the worst blind date I'd ever been on. The last blind date I'd had introduced me to my husband. It was actually pretty uncomfortable, too. But that's a different story.

We brought a miniature photo album with some pictures of our home, our little pet, and us out and about or enjoying our hobbies. Someone had told us that the kids liked that kind of thing. It eased the transition. In retrospect, it was weird. Sight unseen, we showed a little kid photos of a monkey-themed room and a cute dog, and then asked if they wanted to play with it and live with us. This sounds like a kidnapping tactic from the 90s.

We made polite eye contact with the person who brought him in... and then just sort of stared at this kid.

"That's my son," Ryan confirmed. My heart *tried* to see what my husband saw. The boy looked war-torn. He looked like he had no soul. *Really.* There was no sparkle in his eyes. So sad. *Why?*

"What's wrong with that kid?" I wondered.

An agency worker arrived and introduced us to the primary social worker of the boy we were scheduled to meet. Her name was Susan. I think she knew a *lot* more about this boy's story than she would ever reveal. I'll never know, though.

Susan walked over and called this *exact* child out of the crowd. *Really?*

"Steven, come on back," she said. *What* did she say? My husband had an epiphany, but I was confused on multiple levels. I didn't know what to say. Clutching the album, I said nothing. Into a back room, we all went.

Fast forward many months...

My son asked me, "Mommy, did you love me right away?"

My answer is terrible.

"No."

Foster parent training is lacking in many ways. I strongly feel that *all* parents need some form of professional insights and knowledgeable preparation before having kids. I feel like the training we received was sufficient to explain the legalities of fostering and adopting. But I also feel they missed out on counseling foster-adoptive parents' about the impact this journey would have on their hearts.

No one told us to find a counselor or therapist for our own needs. No one told us to begin attending adoption support groups *before* we were in the thick of it. No one told us to start learning about school accommodations or locating other services geared towards foster families, such as respite programs. The end result they encouraged us to achieve was to settle down as a "normal" family.

They told us to keep to our routines and stay small and simple. Physical safety and emotional security for the child was priority number one. Funny, *neither* of those were mentioned in regard to the parents.

When a child comes into the home and is not what you expect, and behaves in very unexpected ways, it affects the parents at a deep level. We experienced shock, fear, isolation, discomfort, disappointment, intrusion, judgment, and much more in such an intense way that our biological parent-friends would never have survived. They told us so.

"I don't know how you do what you do," they'd say. Neither did I.

As the childrens' traumas, pasts, behaviors, and undiagnosed medical conditions are discovered, there is an unraveling. These revelations hit like icy waves against your bones.

There is a sense of deep sadness. But it's *not* regret. At least, it wasn't for us. It was more like, "Oh, so this is how it's going be, huh?" We were never going to go back on our agreement to care for Steven. Giving up simply wasn't an option. Though, I admit, I thought about it many times.

I struggled with post-adoption depression and ended up with my own Post-Traumatic Stress Disorder from the things he put me through.

Sometimes I even hated him. But I never gave up on him.

Imagine with me. Suppose you begin a family by traditional means. You welcome the newborn in and they are beautiful. Apgar scores are great. Then one-month later, you learn that your child can't see well. Is there sadness? Sure. Regret? No. Of course not. You accept your child and all that they come with.

Get them glasses.

That's what a parent does.

And if this happens again next year with a new diagnosis… you accept your child *again*. Then, adjust. It's a no-brainer.

But what if this happens at a rate you cannot compensate for or compartmentalize in order to process?

For a point of reference, the events described in this book regarding Steven happened within a span of ten months. We went from "Hello" to "What the hell?" rather quickly.

Wave after wave, we would be rocked. His story would just keep getting worse.

This resulted in our emotional trauma.

Steven had been living with us for about a month. Things at home weren't settling down as we expected. His erratic behaviors continued to worsen. The more comfortable *he* became, the more we uncomfortable *we* became. Then, it was time for diapers.

"Baby, look at Daddy. Can I see your pretty eyes?" Ryan cajoled the little boy in his arms. Ryan was trying to bond. Steven was trying to eat.

We were informed that sometimes children who have experienced trauma may need to re-live some developmental milestones in order to form a healthy attachment to a caretaker. Depending on when the trauma occurred, you could estimate how far back the child will regress. They said it could be a few years. That sounded alright to me. I could handle a few years.

Well, our kid went back a few *more* years than that.

I think we had heard a sum total of twenty minutes about regressive behavior post-placement. Again, the foster parent training had left us to ride the waves. Or search the Internet.

At this time, I struggled to find a voice online who could tell me "I understand. I've been where you've been. It's going to be okay, and here's some perspective." As it turns out, not very many folks want to talk about their difficult or unusual parenting experiences. Unless you buy their book, of course. *By the way, thanks for buying mine!*

Even then, with a burgeoning bookshelf, I had no real connection to anyone who I could relate to. A how-to solution was one of my least favorite reads because what if *your* how-to was totally ineffective for *me*? Could I get my money back?

Just keep showing them love.

Don't fall in love too fast.

Be consistent.

Be flexible.

I just kept chasing after answers, page-after-page. At the end of the day, I could only do so much. And the little I *could* do was spontaneous, organic, and even a little crazy. It sure *felt* crazy.

Upon Steven's return to our home (after seeing his family for the last time), the hungry boy we met that last week had suddenly become physically and emotionally incapable of feeding himself. To summarize: he needed diapers, he couldn't bathe himself, he couldn't dress himself, and he had forgotten how to use utensils and cups altogether. It was our own personal *Twilight Zone*.

We knew that physically he *could* manage these tasks. We witnessed this for a week. But another something in his brain switched. *Off.*

Steven sat limply at the table and triple-layer sobbed. You know the kind where liquid is coming out of the eyes, the nose, and the mouth?

"I can't!" he'd yell. He wouldn't put any food in his mouth on his own. Nothing we offered him went down. It was time, again, to think fast.

He was psychologically "resetting" his development to the point of his detachment from a primary caretaker. In other words, whenever his biological mother stopped addressing his needs, his mind stuck a bookmark on that page. Upon reaching a place of felt safety, his body remembered where he left off and returned to that point.

What is "felt safety?" It's explicit words and visuals that say "You are safe now." Rules, schedules, and family values provide the structure for this. Moreover, it's implicit messaging ranging from body language to having a full pantry, to clothing that fits, and the freedom to be whomever you want to be. I guess we were able to provide that in short order by staying curious and non-judgmental—for the most part.

And so began his regression. And the bottle feeding. And the potty training. Oh, and school was starting soon. He was supposed to be in second grade this year, but was held back for some reason. There was something mentioned to us about acts of violence... doesn't know his letters… social skill deficits... And now we would be on a deadline to get him back up to speed.

Without a small safety net of caring and understanding people in our lives, this experience would have been embarrassing to a crippling degree. To everyone else, we kept this story a secret.

Our new baby was both verbally and non-verbally asking us to fill-in-the-blanks for some developmental milestones and emotional connections he never received—starting as an infant. Welcome to the world of Attachment Disorders. This sucks. We would now begin a long journey to help re-pattern his thoughts so he could learn to trust a caretaker again.

Since we had no idea at this time there were professionals who could guide the family through this, we just sort of went with it.

By the way, there *are* professionals who can help. They perform attachment therapy. That would have been nice to know in the case this ever happened.

Our job now was to figure out what a baby needed to experience while breastfeeding or bottle feeding. It was an intimate connection with food, touch, smells, and eye contact. That was now the goal.

We started with short sessions. I put a preferred drink in the bottle and had Steven sit near me so our arms or legs could touch. We were silent. There were no expectations of him. I held the bottle out and watched him suck it down with a distant glaze over his eyes. When that was successful, I'd offer him a bottle only while he sat on my lap. The graduation allowed him to continue testing and establishing a sense of felt safety.

We did these little bottle breaks for about a week until he began to relax in my arms and slouch lazily. It wasn't awesome. He was a heavy "baby." And I was just an average 5' 6" build with a yoga hobby (not habit). I wasn't strong by any means. But this was progress!

Once he became comfortable with this process, I started to incorporate talking. I'd say, "Hello," coo and make smiling faces. Yes, just like one would do with an infant. One goal was to provide a feeling of pleasure. The other was to gain eye-contact. That's where deeper bonding could be done.

This isn't just an exercise for the children. This attachment work is beneficial for the parent as well. In these quiet moments, your endorphins are high and you can see visible proof of a connection. Babies turn their face towards yours when you talk. They look all over your face, studying you. Babies memorizing how your lips move, copying your sounds, feeling your nose, grabbing your hair or beard, poking your eyes... these are *precious* memories for the parent.

It was awkward, and not unlike many of the scenes from Robert Munsch's story, *I'll Love You Forever.* But we knew this was what he needed. In fact, I used to sing the song from that book to Steven while we cuddled. It was *exactly* what he needed to hear.

Due to Ryan's job in sales, he was traveling away from the home two weeks out of the month. He missed out on a lot of these "developments." He would come home and I'd do my best to get him caught up to speed. But this phase was particularly tough. Steven would let Ryan bathe him and help him get dressed, but bottle feeding was hard. Steven looked at the ceiling, the fan, the dog, me…

He drank. He laid there. But he wouldn't look at Ryan.

Chapter 4

Reactive Attachment Disorder: My Special Battle

Steven had never formed a healthy attachment to a male parental figure. And it wouldn't end up happening for another four years. Men came and went. Men were "friends." Men did not take care of him.

Whenever Ryan came home from work, it was like the arrival of a celebrity. There was fanfare from a crowd of one. "Daddy's home!!" His peals of joy were like candy-coated poison to me. This response was killing me slowly by intercepting my hormonal and cognitive functions. It looked and sounded like love. What the hell? This kid must have hated me.

"And who am I? Chopped liver?!" I vented to Misty during her weekly visit to our house. She listened calmly with compassion in her eyes. My jealousy was normal. She reminded me that the attachment process for this little boy would take a while.

Later, the psychologists would confirm he had Reactive Attachment Disorder (RAD). This means he either *didn't* form healthy attachments to a caretaker and is now impaired, or he formed unhealthy or maladaptive relationships and is now impaired. This boy experienced both. My husband and I were about to depart from the communal parenting journey and embark on two distinct relational paths with varying timelines: the mother's and the father's.

Steven was showing me how little he needed a mother in his life, despite how desperately he wanted one. Or maybe it was the other way around. Either way, it hurt. And Ryan would be kept in the "friend zone" for years to come, seemingly immune to the targeted tantrums, aggression, and fear-filled reactions. All of that would be specifically (and violently) shared with me for the time being.

Once a certain capacity for trust was established between Steven and me, such as when bathing him or bottle feeding, he would move on to something more difficult. We would be playing "catch up" in his social-emotional development for the foreseeable future. I always felt alone in my struggle. Until a few years later…

At some point, Steven must have realized that my husband wasn't leaving us. He loved Steven. He wanted to adopt Steven from the moment they met. But Steven didn't know what to do with this information. So, he did what worked for him in the past. Steven would begin to "echo" the same dysfunctional behaviors with Ryan, after he and I had achieved mastery. For example, as ten-year-old, Steven was suddenly unable to eat. All. Over. Again. But that time, it *would* be Ryan he looked to.

We were now spoon-feeding Steven. That's not true. It felt much more like force-feeding.

"Close your lips. Chew. Swallow. Swallow it. Come on... let me see? Nope, it's still there. Swallow your food." I negotiated at the beginning. I tried the "One more bite and you get..." game. I made airplane sounds. He hated them.

Since he was old enough to speak, he clarified for me: "I want trains instead!"

Ugh. Trains it was.

We graduated from the bottle to solid foods. Small items. Soft. Like toddlers eat.

"Here comes the choo-choo...! Chugga chugga, into the tunnel." I expected him to open his mouth. Nope. I touched the spoon to his lips and tried to part them. Nope. The teeth gates were closed. But I was using a train, *like he asked.*

Steven would not eat. It was the classic struggle with a toddler. But, he was a big toddler. Thankfully, he ate out with friends. He ate the church refreshments. He ate when Grandma was here. And he was doing "fine" on the outside. But if I, the M-O-M, touched his food, he shut down.

This was my special battle.

I recently asked my son about his memory of these events. The little devil grinned from ear to ear. "Why didn't you eat my food?" I asked. It was simple. He knew.

"I didn't trust you." *Noted.*

"Do you remember the green beans?" I pushed.

Yes, he did. His grin was now an open-mouthed laugh.

I cooked green beans. They were soft and chopped small. He was doing better with things like mashed potatoes and grapes. He liked butter and salt like it was the magical key to gustatory admission.

I was figuring this out. Or, I thought I was.

"Here comes the choo-choo..." Again. Up the hill. Down the hill. And into the tunnel? *Yes!* He opened up.

I tucked the little bean inside with the fork and scraped it off using his teeth. It immediately rolled right back out of his mouth and onto his lap.

I set the fork down, muttered an "oops" of sorts and picked up the bean with my fingers.

"Try again," I said. I pushed my fingers through his lip seal and ran into that tooth gate again.

"Open," I commanded, knowing that he could very likely bite me. But he didn't—this time. He turned his head to the left, tilted back, and arched his body.

Breakfast had been a cereal disaster. He spat his milk out like a fire hose. Lunch wasn't any better. A cheese stick and banana. At least both could be mashed and scooped off the chin to be re-mashed through the gaps in his teeth.

I knew he was hungry. I knew it tasted good. *Just eat the green bean, son!*

Standing up, I could meet his impending conniptions, jerk for jerk.

He thrashed to the right and said, "Uh-uh" (no).

I brought the green bean over and said, "Uh-huh" (yes).

I used my free hand to pry open the side section of his teeth. Just a little more and I could pop the greeny in.

"Bleah! I don't want it!" Steven pulled it out and threw the green bean across the dining room.

Fine. There's more where that came from.

"You need to eat," I reasoned. He started with the tears. I picked up another projectile and faced him.

"Open up."

"Noooo!" Perfect. He opened his mouth to scream at me. That was my opportunity. I popped the bean in and then covered his open mouth to prevent it from falling out. Now he bit.

"Ow!"

And spit and drooled. He mashed that green bean up and pushed it's liquified contents through my fingers. *Ew.* Win for Steven.

"Don't forget the part where I called you a B-word," my son informed me matter-of-factly. Yep, that's right. We couldn't *possibly* leave that part out.

Thirty minutes of falling out of his chair, crawling under the table, back up onto his chair, all utensils were forgone and there was more food on our clothing than on the table... His tears had dried up and been replaced by murderous lasers.

"Swallow." I tried again. He had something in his mouth. Only God knew what it was at this point.

A familiar rattling sound came from the front door. Keys in the lock. Daddy was home.

With one quick gulp, Steven sat up straight and wiped his face. "Hi, Daddy! How was your day?"

That's it. I needed a drink.

Later that evening, he would help himself to a basket of "anytime" food that we set out on the counter. Because he was so hungry and foraged when no one was looking, we tried to get one step ahead. In this basket were crackers, fruit, nuts, granola bars and other grab-and-go snacks.

"Steven, you can eat this anytime you need to. You don't have to steal food in this house. You will always have food to eat." We found wrappers under his bed, hidden in his laundry basket, or inside pants pockets. He still felt the need to hide this behavior from us.

Food insecurity was expected, based on his past. We were taught about this behavior in foster parent training. Some people put locks on the refrigerator and pantry to manage the eating. No snacks between meals. Going hungry between meals was normal. The result would be better eating habits at mealtimes. I could see the logic in this.

We had also heard of another approach. I think it was a solid piece of advice from Mr. Wells regarding felt safety.

"*Show him* that food is always available. *Show him* that he will never go hungry again, no matter what."

And not unlike leaving cookies out for Santa, the basket would "mysteriously" go empty, and be refilled regularly.

Now we had food insecurity, layered with regression, layered further with an attachment disorder. The digestive problems would also continue for a while.

"Sweetie, when *did* you learn to trust me?" Our recent conversation continued. I thought I could get some insights for this book.

Steven replied, "Yesterday."

So much for that.

Chapter 5

Bedtime: When No One Sleeps

(GASP.) What now? The glow from the baby monitor lit up our bedroom. I looked at the clock on my phone. 4:00 a.m.

Whimpers and soft sobs barely registered through the speaker.

Please. Go back to sleep. Mommy is tired.

"Steven, it's okay. You're safe. I'm right here. I can hear you," I cooed softly into the monitor. I didn't want to wake Ryan up since he had a long day of work ahead. *As if I didn't.*

"Baby, do you need me?" *Say no.* I crossed my fingers, but he cried louder. Okay. Time to get up. Again.

The first time was at 10:00 p.m. Then 12:30 a.m. Again at 2:30 a.m. to go to the bathroom. Those were the easy nights.

Falling asleep was hard for Steven. The bedtime routine was long. Bath, stories, cuddles, back rubs, songs... then my silent retreat towards the door. One step. Two steps.

"Momma?" *Ah! No, Baby. No...*

"Yes, Baby?" He was scared. Could I leave the light on? Could I keep the door open? Could I rub his back again? Could he have another blanket? Could I sleep with him? Could he sleep with me?

We were still in the toddler phase. Potty training. Feeding. And sleep training.

Okay, okay... "Just one more hug."

And a kiss. And another. Okay just *five* more. *Sheesh!*

"It's like I can never give him enough kisses," I explained to Misty. It was weird. He only asked for them at nighttime. During the day, we barely touched outside of pure function. He seemed scared of my touch. In fact, the first time I ever placed my hand on his skin for more than a hot second was to apply sunblock at the pool. If I ever raised my hand for anything, he'd shrink like a battered puppy. Sometimes this would come with a breathy, "Don't hit me!" *What the...? Was he serious?* I was just going to brush his hair.

For the next five years, he'd have an automatic, "I'm sorry, please don't hit me," reaction when anything went wrong. If he answered a math question wrong. If he spilled his water cup. If he didn't know where his shoes were. He expected to be hit. All. The. Time. The flinch was ingrained.

We've managed to help him drop the second part by explaining that he'd be giving other people reason to believe we were the parents who abused him. *Yeah kid, take it down a notch.*

The "My mom does drugs" story he told was also a high priority for re-wording.

Misty responded. "Right. You'll *never* be able to give him enough. That's part of his story." Her explanation confused me.

Steven needed a mom so much that the need *was* insatiable. He didn't just need a hug and a kiss for that night, but he needed and wanted one for the last thousand or so nights before living with us. He needed *those* kisses too.

One thing that has stuck out for me in these long, trying nights was that he never cried out for *his* mother. As in his biological mother. No "I-want-my-mommy" moments to make me think this was a simple case of homesickness. Reflecting on this knowledge makes me sad. For her. I never thought I'd say those words.

Though I loved feeling needed and being on the receiving end of his affection, this was an odd situation to be in. All day long, I was feared and hated. All night long, he sought after me. I was getting whiplash at this point.

"Should we try co-sleeping? It feels like we can't ever get through the night," I asked Misty.

She was careful with her response. "I know that can be helpful in many situations. But having the child sleep in your room or in your bed is strictly against foster care rules. I'm sorry." *Oh. I see.*

So, I started sleeping in his room.

He'd wake still. After finding me on the floor and whispering "Hi, Mom," we could connect briefly without anyone getting out of bed at all.

"Hi, Baby. I'm still here. Did you have a bad dream? Want me to rub your head?" Mumbling into my pillow without lifting an eyelid was *so* much better. I could even reach his head from where I was on the floor. *There, there... go back to sleep.*

After a minute or two, I'd roll over and hope it worked. He must have thought I was asleep already when he whispered, "I just love you so much."

Really? My heart warmed. But as I held my breath and listened further, he squeezed and kissed his stuffed animal.

"Good night, Beary," he'd say.

Oh. He meant the doll. *Ow.*

Some nights were worse. And it didn't matter where I slept.

3:00 a.m.

"Pew! Pew! Pew!" Heavy breathing accompanied little fingers clenching into fists.

"Pew! Pew!" Those were the gunshot sounds.

"No!" He would whimper, roll into the fetal position and gasp. I couldn't tell if he was crying or trying to fight back. He started pounding his fists on the pillow.

It was time to go get him.

I've had the unfortunate "privilege" of witnessing him covering his face, slamming his head into the bed over and over, or even slapping himself... The universal gestures of "make it stop!" By the time I arrived, he was drenched in sweat and the backs of his hands were slicked from wiping tears.

Steven once told me that sleeping is "when all the bad things happen." In his mind, of course.

"Sweetie, I'm here. What's wrong?" I'd ask. He didn't know. Sometimes he would push me away and tell me to leave him alone. Sometimes he'd cry more once I arrived. Sometimes he laid awake, lost in his head, not even aware of my presence. Whatever experience he was reliving was outside of my reach. *So much fear!* What happened to him?

I don't know what his exposure to gun violence was. It wasn't in the paperwork. *Of course not.* It may have been a one-time event of extreme terror. Or it may have been a recurring theme based on the criminal records I found through an Internet search. That's one way to outsmart the system: Google people.

Either way, the panic he felt when triggered manifested in many ways, one being

nightmares reliving the same scenario repeatedly. Always waking up scared. Always gunshots. Always trying to get away.

These episodes would lead us to a diagnosis of Post-Traumatic Stress Disorder (PTSD). I recognized these nighttime events from my experience with my grandfather. My grandfather is a WWII veteran. A bomber pilot. He had bad nightmares, too.

After all of that, Steven could not go back to sleep. Didn't want to.

No sleep aid could stop the ghosts of torture haunting our household at night. No oil, scent, herb, or sound machine worked. None of it. It took him a full six months before he slept through an entire night. *Me too.*

The exhaustion took its toll on us.

Chapter 6

Is It Okay To Be Afraid?

F*or the life of* me, I don't remember what set him off. When Steven got mad, he got violent. And destructive. And injurious.

Stomping and yelling evolved into kicking the wall. Once, he bit a hole in the drywall. A logistical feat, for sure.

That day, I stood my ground on whatever issue had come up. Steven wasn't pleased. He ran upstairs and grabbed a framed picture of the family from his bedroom. Coming back out, he didn't even take a beat before hurling it over the railing to crash onto the tile floor below.

"...Then, I'm leaving! I hate you and I hate living here. You're the *worst* mom. You never listen!" He ran back in for another framed photo. (*CRASH.*)

I continued to stand my ground. This wasn't the first time we'd been down this road. Each explosion could last between an hour and four. And he always saved them for a time when Ryan wasn't around or on a work trip. Like now.

I wasn't just losing my mind at *this* point—it had been gone for a while. *I was so tired.*

The growling began.

He used to growl like a wild animal. It wasn't like most kids play-acting. It was primal and sounded painful.

I remember walking up the stairs, ignoring the broken photos for the moment.

Walking past him on the landing, I went into his room and looked for any other photos remaining. *There's one.* It was a baby photo we received from his relatives. I'm not proud of my choice, but it had a frame and glass, so I picked it up and returned to the landing.

He looked back and forth between the photo and I. His eyes widened.

"You're not the only one who can break things," I said. And over it went.

Fueled with a new fury, he railed. "You can't do that. That was MINE!"

Fists clenched, he came at me. No, not like a toddler tantrum. Like somebody who has witnessed these moves before, practiced for a time when he would need them, and was now showing the world how he *would have* stood up for himself in the past. But now he was bigger and stronger.

This wasn't the first time he'd violently attack me. Or the last. Biting, kicking, hitting, scratching, and my least favorite; head banging. When he threw his head back, I was preoccupied with trying to stop the assault from other directions. *If I could just hold this hand down and keep that leg from...* "Oh! Oww!!" Tears welled up. He got my chin and nose "right on the money," as they say.

Before this, I had never been hit. No violent hand was ever laid to my flesh.

To be clear, I was spanked by both of my parents for being a total brat as a child. First, I had to sit through a Bible lesson or lecture about *why* what I did or said was wrong in the eyes of the Lord. Then, some arbitrary number of swats was delivered.

I never feared a spanking.

I walked away thinking that I'd trade more swats, for fewer sermons *any day.*

Releasing the feisty whips, I made a dash to distance myself. My head hurt. My arm hurt worse, though.

A recent injury left me with a loss of strength, accompanied by constant nerve pain in my arm. Steven knew this. He knew I was weak. Defending myself came at an agonizing cost.

He growled again, set his jaw, and looked me in the eye. *What in the world...?*

Then he took a fist to his own face.

Holy cow. I had never seen anything like this before.

"Steven, no! Stop that!" He gathered his strength and hit again—this time up by his temple.

This reminded me of those ancient warriors who beat themselves with sticks in order to "toughen up" before battle. Whatever expression crossed my face... whatever tone was in my voice... I'll never know if he liked it or disliked it. The result was another blow to the opposite side of his head.

What do I do?

Scared, both for him and myself at this point, I ran to my room and slammed the door. Steven roared louder. Closed doors—especially locked ones—incited *more* fear and anger.

He was already at the door handle as I fumbled to secure the lock against *his* efforts. My fingers screamed in pain. It wasn't enough for me to just lock my bedroom door. I had to go deeper.

I went into the closet and fell apart. The boy's screams coming from outside my room were tormenting me. You wouldn't have believed the thoughts running through my head… even if I told you. And I will.

For a moment, let's set aside the fact that this was a child. Steven was a person whom I did not have a trusting relationship with. He had been in my home for a very short time, uninvited (*almost*), was now destroying my property, using force on me, threating to hurt me more, chasing after me, and trying to break into my locked bedroom doors. We can add to this fact that we recently discovered that this person (i.e. my attacker) had a prior history of violence, including a pencil stabbing. *Yeah.* Anything could quickly become a weapon in his hands.

For many readers, these context clues might help you understand why I feared for my life. I wanted to kill him. For every blow he delivered, I wanted to fight back. For every curse and threat, I was ready to choke the life out of him. Ball kicks, eye gouges, the broken glass… I wanted to do it all. No one, and I mean *no one,* was permitted to attack me like this and live. *Right?*

Fear and fatigue were scrambling my thoughts! These were *not* the thoughts of a mother about her child. These thoughts were not allowed. But he was *not* my child. He was an outsider. *Could I shoot him through the door?*

I let out a wretched howl of my own and the ugly crying began. *What was happening?*

As a foster parent, there was a strict protocol for this type of event. Absolutely no hand of violence must be laid on this child. That would land me a holiday in jail. And he'd end up… God knows where.

Blinking against tears, I knew I needed to make a call. 9-1-1, I dialed. *This is crazy, right?* I pushed the call button. *This is crazy!*

"Operator, What's the emergency?" Her crystal clear voice was steady, unlike my hands. I wasn't sure what to say.

"Hi, um. I have a little boy." Duh. What was the emergency? My brain tried to organize the details faster than my mouth could produce the words.

"He's from foster care." *Like that explained it all.*

"He…" *How do I put it?* "He's trying to hurt me."

Thank God for these operators. I know she'd probably heard much worse in her career. And perhaps, she's even heard the same story at some point. Without a beat, she proceeded with the essentials: Where are you right now? Where is he? Does he have a weapon?

Ohmygod… Thankfully, or perhaps hopefully, I responded, "No."

Assured we were both alive, the operator asked, "Would you like me to send the police out?" They could restrain him—with force, if necessary. I paused.

"I don't know." He's *just* a child. He's an angry little boy who has been through hell. And what am I, the adult, doing here? Did I really need the police to come? Was it *really* that bad? I doubted myself. I didn't know what the right thing to do was.

These doubting thoughts were spoken by others as well: anyone who I happened to slip a detail to. Ever-so-often, someone would ask me how things were going with the new child. Depending on my mood, or the events of that morning, my typical "fine" filter might have short-circuited. Oh, these bruises? That hole in the wall? Ah. Yeah, my kid attacked me. You know how it goes.

If an outsider heard about the way my son behaved, I would get reactive comments like, "Yikes! Then why don't you tell CPS to take him back?"

Or the judgmental, "I would *never* put up with that. Spank his ass. Show him who's boss."

Or the know-it-all, "Yeah, I've heard about kids like that. Didn't you know what you were getting into? Don't they prepare you for this stuff?"

No. *NO THEY DON'T!* I wanted to scream.

He was still in attack mode.

"I'm gonna KILL YOU!" Steven raged outside my bedroom. He kicked at the door. Punched. Repeatedly. The hinges and handle rattled against his efforts.

"Ma'am?" The operator repeated herself. "Do you want us to send the police out?"

With one more roar, Steven charged my door. *"Raaaah...!"* (*THUNK!*) Silence.

"Uh. Hold on. He just stopped." I told her. I looked out from my closet at the bedroom door and swallowed hard.

Standing up and walking quietly toward the doors, I listened again. Twisting the doorknob and opening it a small way to assess the situation, I found Steven curled into a ball, panting and squeaking breathlessly in pain. He was holding his head.

He must have taken a charge into the door head first, like that bald-looking dinosaur with a hard head.

Looking up at me, all prior demons exorcized, he chattered out, "Ow, Mommy! My head!"

Even with his arms now reaching out to me for help, I hesitated. *Don't touch me.*

"He hit his head. Really hard," I reported to the operator. She transferred me to some type of medical responder. As I watched the boy's rage transform into shock, pain, and helplessness, a new woman walked me through checking for the signs of a concussion. I looked him over curiously. I was worried about him, but at the same time bizarrely fascinated at his sudden need for my attention. How long would this last? How much more time until the *next* round began?

"Mommy, help me," he cried. I kept my distance; touching only what was necessary to complete the injury assessment. No signs of a concussion.

Dutifully, I repeated back all the instructions on observing him and seeking follow up care. After thanking the medical personnel, I ended the call and stepped away from Steven.

A high pitch tone was migrating from one side of my brain to the other. I was flatlining. Emotionally, that is. I'd been drained of every last thing I could possibly feel for this child. Knowing he was medically safe, I took one last look at him on the floor of the hallway. *This is crazy.*

Spinning on my heel, I went back to my room and closed the door behind me. Safe in the closet once more, I sat in shock—wounded and utterly exhausted.

Before I called the social worker to file another incident report, I needed to talk to my husband.

"Please… Can you come home? I'm scared," I begged him through my sobs. Knowing full well what doing so would cost him at his job, Ryan canceled the remainder of his work trip. *That's* the kind of guy he is. Mr. Wells was wrong to doubt him.

Reflecting on this story with my son, he remembered none of it. Not a single moment.

Steven appeared sad, so I asked, "What do you think?"

In a moment of clarity, he said, "I broke you." Well put. *Yes, you did, Baby. Yes, you did.*

"Anything else?" I continued.

"It's a Pachycephalosaurs." What? Oh. The dinosaur.

It was my turn to laugh.

"Yes, Son. That was the *exact* animal you portrayed." Homeschooling science lessons were paying off.

Chapter 7

Can Love Really Change People?

We needed answers.

What was going on with Steven? He was devolving before our eyes.

I took him in for an emergency psychiatric evaluation. We had to do *something*. Reporting these events to Child Protective Services or the police simply wasn't enough. They had no solutions! CPS thanked me for the information regarding his attacks. *Um, you're welcome?*

The police acted like, "What do you want *us* to do, ma'am? He's *your* child."

On another occasion, I asked for the police to come out and just talk to my son about his violence. They sounded confused, "Do you want to press charges?"

"No, just come talk to him. Help him to understand how serious this is and how scary the consequences are..." I was grasping at this point. Somebody, please *do something!*

The officer interrupted me. "Ma'am, we don't come out to scare children. You should take him to a psychiatrist."

I thought for sure the psych ward would keep him there, considering he was a danger to both himself and me. But they determined that he was now sound of mind and had not *consciously* attempted to hurt me.

The attack might have been what some refer to as a "blackout rage." This meant that his stress hormone cortisol and blood pressure were so highly escalated, it disrupted normal brain function. He had no idea what he was doing. This worried me.

I worried about him going to school. I worried about him in church, on the playground, and while playing at the neighbor's house. What if he attacks others? I thought, "This kid is going to end up in jail, someday." Or worse.

The ER doctor suggested Steven might have Oppositional Defiance Disorder, or Post-Traumatic Stress Disorder, or simply anxiety. They referred us out for a follow-up with a local psychologist. *Thanks, Doc. That's super conclusive.*

Steven was prescribed sedatives—a lot of them. I wasn't pleased. I did not want to sedate a child. To me, it was a band-aid for a much deeper issue. At this point, I'd called everyone and reported everything, but it felt like *no one* was listening and *no one* cared. At least, no one did as much as I did.

Misty empathized with me. "Steven is in *such* good care. Your advocating for him is what he needs, as well as all the nurturing, caring, and consistency you and Ryan are providing. What a great gift you are to him. And he, to you."

She always had a way with words. And she reminded me that someone *did* care. Someone cared about Steven a lot.

But caring for Steven challenged me. Didn't he *just* attack me? Why would I go through all this trouble for a child who could never possibly love me in return?[4]

"You have a strong sense of justice," Misty observed.

Part of me felt relieved Steven wasn't truly trying to kill me. But another part grieved. The diagnoses we would receive could not possibly encapsulate the impact of his (then) lifelong trauma. Whatever happened in his life before living with us damaged him. Whoever he was with… whatever he saw or heard… it was enough to alter his brain function!

My gut reaction was to help him. *I had to.* And my only rationale for this was some crazy inner drive that defied the fact that this child was not even mine. Though, I continued to act as-if he was. It was becoming my automatic response.

My grandfather, the pilot, and my grandmother were foster-to-adopt parents in the 50's. Sixty years later, I asked my grandfather if he had ever felt something like I did with the children he had. His answer surprised me.

"I loved them," Grandpa told me. "Every single one."

He still thought of them. He even included them in his family photo albums, though every single child was adopted out to some other family. They didn't even have the chance to keep one. I know that hurt him.

Well, crap. This entire situation with Steven was built on a foundation of errors and broken policies. He wasn't a good match for us on paper. If, in advance, we had known a fraction of the things we

4 "But God showed His great love for us by sending Christ to die for us while we were still sinners." (Romans 5:8, The Living Bible)

learned once he came to live with us, we would have hung up on Mr. Wells's call. *Next!*

I started to have long conversations with God over how this would play out. What did we get ourselves into? And what should we do now? I questioned Him many times.[5]

Even though we had no guarantee that Steven would remain in our home for *any* known amount of time, I was getting attached. *Don't get attached!*

I tried to convince myself that it was unwise to go all-in so fast. It could potentially result in heartbreak. *Right?* That's a logical path.

He might not be staying. Don't let this hurt. Keep the kid at arm's length. Maybe he *would* leave, and we'd try again for a different child. One who better suited us.

Ouch. That hurt to put into words.

This attitude is only a sliver of what many children in foster care feel. These children move from home to home, but not one of the families is "theirs."

"*He's not mine*," echoed in my mind.

It's all temporary. Acting out just buys the kids a ticket to another new home. We were Steven's seventh. Foster children typically have little-to-no personal possessions. They struggle to settle into a school. They don't always receive consistent medical care. And most try not to let people into their hearts.

---

5 1. "Jesus replied, 'You don't understand now what I am doing, but someday you will.'" (John 13:7, New Living Translation)
2. "For just as the heavens are higher than the earth, so My ways are higher than your ways and My thoughts higher than your thoughts. (Isaiah 55:9, New Living Translation)

When everyone in your life "leaves," or disappoints you, it's a natural response to build a protective wall around your heart. *"Don't let him hurt you..."*

Children stuck in the revolving door, like Steven was, tend to stop relying on people. They stop trusting. And they stop connecting. It's a necessary function to survive in this transient situation.

But was this a necessary attitude for *me* to have? What else did I have to be afraid of?

Oh.

I considered what it would be like to have Steven's social worker make a carefully worded call to me announcing she'd found a "perfect" family match for him. Steven would leave my home within five days—the standard notification period for a removal. It gave me pause. (More like, it choked me.) I couldn't let that to happen. *I think I love him, too, Grandpa.*

I didn't know how to enjoy loving Steven, yet. You could say my "love language" was to perform acts of service. It was the easiest way. Besides, he wasn't exactly an affectionate child.

For me, loving this boy was more like being on a mission. Some called it heroic: "You are such a saint for taking that boy in!" Some called it a waste of time: "Why would you go through all that effort for a *foster kid*?" Plus, we'd been having more bad days than good at that point. It was a confusing time.

To hold, feed, and cuddle the squirmy kiddo that hated on me constantly was hard. I'd put up with tears, self-harm, and destruction to the furniture, yard, carpets, and more. The constant battles made it difficult to keep my energy in the black.

I know I said this book wasn't for giving advice, but here, I can't stop myself. Spousal support while fostering is just as critical as maintaining a relationship to a higher spiritual power. These connections were my lifelines. Without Ryan reminding me I was a good mother, and that I wasn't alone, it might have been too much.

Spouses, *please*, pour into each other daily. Remind each other how much the other matters, and that you are a team on this journey.

Your spouse came before the child, is here with the child, and (God-willing) will remain after the child has grown and gone. Hold on to each other and don't lose faith in love. When you see the other person slipping into the darkness, go pull them out. Even if you are a single parent on this journey, for every "I am hated" thought that the child provokes, follow this up with some sort of reflection on how much you *are* loved by those in your inner circle.

Knowing you are still capable of loving and are lovable in return is one way to stay afloat when the waves of disappointment or fear hit. For me, in addition to Ryan, I am assured that God always had been, currently is, and will forever be a part of our adoption story. God's love sustained me.[6]

In this book, I make several references to many unintentional and unapproved events which occurred. But there is one thing I would never call them: *accidental.* I believe parents are carefully

6 "For God did not give us a spirit of fear, but of power, love, and a sound mind." (2nd Timothy 1:17, New Heart English Version)

selected.[7] This is evidenced in many stories in the Bible. Mary[8], Elizabeth, Rachel, and Hannah come to mind easily as mothers, though there are numerous divine fatherships as well. In short, I believe God knew (more than I) that I had what it would take to become Steven's mom.

A parent's specific skills and personality can shape their children and direct them to fulfill a God-given purpose. Some call this a hope or a wish. I believe it's all part of God's plan. In other words, one's life experiences, inner drives, passions, and weaknesses are all resources we can draw upon to become the perfect parent for the child that arrives in our lives.

God's methods, though often mysterious to us, are perfect in timing and execution.[9] God was there on the day I pulled the car off the road to answer the phone. Only the details about Steven that we would say "yes" to were made available. *Hmm.* Looking back, that makes me chuckle.

God was present in the family services room where we all met. He drew Ryan's heart to a child immediately. And, I believe God's plans for this boy and I are good.[10] He placed a child with a fighting spirit alongside a mother who knew how to win fights. (I'll explain

---

7 "No one has ever seen God; but if we love one another, God lives in us and love is made complete in us." (1st John 4:12, New Living Translation)

8 Mary is the mother of Jesus (Luke 1:26-38). Elizabeth is the mother of John the Baptist (Luke 1:5-17). Rachael is the mother of King Joseph (Genesis 30:22-24). Hannah is the mother of King Samuel. (1st Samuel, Chapter 1).

9 "As for God, His ways are perfect. The Lord's word is flawless; He shields all who take refuge in Him." (Psalms 18:30, New Living Translation)

10 "For I know the plans I have for you," declares the Lord, "plans to prosper you and not to harm you, plans to give you hope and a future." (Jeremiah 29:11, New International Version)

this soon.) And *that* mother would eventually discover how to harness his weaknesses and transform them into assets. I believe that now, with all my heart.

But it took time to see things through God's eyes. It was hard to see God's promises being fulfilled while still in the middle of the storms. Frankly, it was and is still much easier to find comfort knowing my husband was on the life raft with me as we were being tossed to and fro'.[11]

Children learn *how* to love and be loved by following the examples of their parents. The caveat to this is, even as foster (ie. provisional) parents, we should not take an unattached, arms-length approach to parenting. Loving Steven transformed him. It enabled him to become the sweet, highly intelligent boy we know him to be now.

By showing the child what it means to love, parents create a deeper sense of felt safety.[12] They hear *how* you speak to your family. They see *how* you touch and hug. By observing you relate to, lift up, and depend on your spouse, they learn. And then the day will come when they can feel safe and ready to imitate what they've witnessed. This happens in rapid fashion to the majority of neuro-typical children raised by their biological parents.

In our case, this learning process was disrupted. But Steven's ability to learn was not ruined. Brains are flexible (neuroplastic). Ryan and I had innumerable opportunities to model a new way of

---

11 1st John, Chapter 4, Verse 12: "No one has ever seen God; but if we love one another, God lives in us and love is made complete in us." (Holy Bible, New Living Translation)

12 "Whoever fears the Lord has a secure fortress, and for their children, it will be a refuge." (Psalms 127: 3-5, New Living Translation)

relating and responding to people. Healing would come from *our* habits.

I also needed to practice a new way of responding to Steven. When motivated by fear or anger, my actions can be defensive and spiteful. Put another way, doing the right thing for the wrong reasons, is still wrong. And it impacts the relationship.

For example, walking away from Steven after his attack did no outward harm to him or me. It provided physical safety. But it left us disconnected and emotionally unavailable to each other. This makes healing harder. Perhaps, after his rage, I could have held him and said that Mommy knows what it's like to have big feelings, and I can help him to not hurt people or get himself hurt next time. The latter action is driven by love and a desire to *remain* connected, whereas the former is motivated by fear.[13]

This connection-mentality can also help foster parents maintain a sense of inner peace. As an example, when Steven shoves his dinner plate across the table and screams, my response *could* be driven by anger. Thoughts of "*Not again!*" might result in me plopping Steven onto my lap and (force) feeding him. If I consciously choose love as my motive to act, I might respond differently.[14]

"Sweetie, I know the potato is hot. Let's blow on it first and try again." Then, I'd still sit with him on my lap and feed him. There is

---

13 "Fathers, do not provoke your children to anger by the way you treat them. Rather, bring them up with the discipline and instruction that comes from the Lord." (Ephesians 6:4, New Living Translation)

14 "Love is patient, love is kind. It does not envy, it does not boast, it is not proud. It does not dishonor others, it is not self-seeking, it is not easily angered, it keeps no record of wrongs. Love does not delight in evil but rejoices with the truth. It always protects, always trusts, always hopes, always perseveres. Love never fails." (1st Corinthians 13:4-8, New International Version)

virtually no difference in the two resulting actions. But there is a distinct difference in how the motives impact tone, patience, energy, and our connection to each other. This is the higher road we must take in order to build trust.

Steven used to fight me when I tried to hold his hand. At first, I forced the issue as a matter of safety. Crossing roads, boarding a subway, or navigating crowded places *required* hand-holding. That didn't stop him from pulling away from me, though.

Remember: *being* safe and *feeling* safe are different things.

Then, one day, we had a breakthrough. Ryan, Steven, and I had gone to the beach.

"We were on a field trip!" my son recalled. His joy in hearing this story being told speaks volumes.

Ryan and I took turns taking a picture with Steven in front of an ocean backdrop. Steven stood on a short wall that separated beach from boardwalk. He put his hand on Ryan's shoulder and stood nice and tall. They were a handsome couple.

When it was my turn, I sat on the wall next to Steven and I asked if I could pose holding his hand. He gave it to me! Turning to smile at the camera, I felt like I had just won the lottery.

Chapter 8

Pushing Back Against The System

F*ueled with a new* sense of purpose, we began digging further into Steven's mental and physical health. Unfortunately, as foster parents, we were not granted full legal rights to manage his medical care.

This meant that we could not rightfully take him off the medications he was being prescribed. We could not access his prior medical records outside of what the social worker initially told us. And we had to get permission from a judge to make any changes or additions to his treatment plans. The red tape was thick. And sticky. I had to make do with whatever I could and beg doctors to listen to my notes. *Or break more rules and just stop giving him the sedative, anyway.*

I started journaling the blackout events, their frequency, and the potential triggers. I became a web sleuth and read more books about disorders associated with trauma. It was all rather complicated. Symptoms overlapped.

I could understand why the doctors could easily give him multiple diagnoses, or even conflicting ones. Or flat-out wrong ones. Like epilepsy. *Yeah.* Steven experienced seizures for the first year and a half he was with us. It's unclear how long he'd been having them before us. Or what the true cause was. I suspected stress.[15]

While the doctors toyed with prescription cocktails, Ryan and I were performing our own series of experiments at home. At one point, we adjusted Steven's diet. No more gluten! No more dairy! Dairy had an impact, gluten didn't.

We tried a variety of supplements such as biotin, fish oil, and melatonin. We adjusted his sleep schedule, activities, and screen time. Honestly, some trials were pulled out of thin air. Some were suggestions from well-intending friends. But my favorite resources were actually other parent's memoirs.

I read book after book from parents of adopted or special needs children. The authors were some of the wisest people I knew at the time. They translated parenting How-To books into a reality for me. I saw myself in their shoes and heard my child's story through theirs.

One thing resonated in each parent's story: tenacity. The families that "made it," were the families that never gave up on their children

---

15 Similar to Post-Traumatic Stress Disorder, or perhaps, a comorbid disorder, is the presence of Psychogenic Non-Epileptic Seizures (PNES). These are "episodes of altered movement, sensation, or experience that mimic epileptic seizures, but are not caused by abnormal brain activity and are assumed to reflect an emotional disorder. … Reports of psychologically traumatic events, such as physical or sexual abuse, are commonly cited as integral to the genesis of PNES behavior."

Testa, M., Krauss, G., Lesser, R., and Brandt, J. "Stressful life event appraisal and coping in patients with psychogenic seizures and those with epilepsy." *Seizure-Journal.com* 21.4 (2012) 282-287. Seizure. Web. 2019, Jan. 29

or their marriage. Parents who studied their children instead of fearing or judging, became vastly equipped to raise them successfully. In many cases, they ended up knowing more than their children's doctors and defying the odds.

I was determined to join the ranks.

Steven was a zombie when I picked him up from school one day. Totally distant. He barely spoke other than babbling sounds. He ate dinner as if he hadn't eaten all day.

Something was wrong.

I held an impromptu after-school meeting with Steven's new teacher, Mrs. Edward.

"Something is happening at school. I'm worried about Steven. He comes home with limited brain function, it seems. Can you tell me what you've seen?"

Her response was not what I expected. "Steven has been rather defiant and stubborn. I asked him to do something and he yelled, 'I said NO!' to me." *Really?* He yelled at the teacher? I mean, sure, he's been yelling at *me*, but everyone else tells me how he is so well-behaved. I almost don't believe them. But that day, I *definitely* didn't believe her.

She reported further, "He goofs off when he is supposed to be working. He acts like he forgot the instructions, even immediately after I've said them. Then, he interrupts the class by asking for help *all the time*!"

For a moment, I forgot that it was me who initiated this meeting to resolve some problems we saw after school. Apparently, I was now in a Parent-Teacher Conference where my child's performance was a target, instead of a goal.

"Oh, okay. I'm sorry to hear this," I responded. "What area is he struggling in? What does he need help with?"

"Nothing. He's just trying to get attention." Or in other words, she didn't know. Or care.

Steven had only been in school for about a month when he was removed from his study group table and given a single desk against the back wall of the room. Alone. Like a dunce. He didn't know why. I looked at his pathetic desk setup and asked, "What does he need to do to rejoin the others?"

"Stop interrupting," Mrs. Edward put simply. "He has to stop distracting the class and follow directions." So, she wanted him to be quiet.

But what's a kid to do when he can't see the whiteboard? We were still in the process of getting him glasses. His latest ophthalmologist visit flagged one of his eyes with 80% vision loss. For a reference, 85% is considered full blindness.

And what's he supposed to do when he doesn't know what the instructions on his page say? I'm pretty sure I mentioned that he didn't know all his letters yet...

Worse, what if he has a bowel sensation and needs to go to the bathroom more than once in the hour? The day he came home incoherent, I sent a note along with Steven about his stomach pains and "other symptoms." I thought I had gone over this with Mrs. Edward previously, as well. Steven was supposed to be seated near the door so he could get to the bathroom quickly.

I got an e-mail response to my note:

> *"I received your note regarding the stomachache, but Steven did not appear to be in any pain. He was actually smiling and excited to begin the day. During PE, he ran around and played without complaint. Just before lunch recess, I asked him how his stomach felt. He said it hurt, so I walked him to the office to sit instead of playing. It is common to hear students say they have a stomachache when it is time to do something they don't enjoy, like reading lab or math centers." ...Or recess?*

She thought he was trying to go to the bathroom as an excuse to get out of schoolwork. This wouldn't be the only type of accident the teacher would let go unaddressed.

"Mommy?" Steven was shy and embarrassed. I told him he could say anything he needed to say. "Can I try wearing diapers... at school?" *Oh, man.* We made a compromise. He would now carry a spare set of underwear and pants at the bottom of his backpack.

Eventually, I noticed a pattern in the teacher's reports. Steven complained "so much," that he was being held back from recess day ...after day ... after day. She had tried giving him time-outs for his disruptive behavior.

But *then* we were told, "He returns back to the same antics immediately. He will be losing whole recess periods for his behaviors from now on."

It was becoming clear to us that this teacher was ill-equipped to address Steven's needs in addition to the other twenty-plus children at the same time. She was treating him as a classic troublemaker.

Well, since we weren't going to get anywhere with Mrs. Edward, I asked Steven about these issues.

"Sweetie, why don't you play outside at recess?"

"I don't know. I have to sit in the room instead."

"Did you yell at your teacher?"

Yes. She didn't hear him the first time he spoke… so he spoke louder and was punished.

Dear Mrs. Edward, When you put a child against the back wall, it becomes harder for them to hear you, and you them… I think she was lacking common sense. This wasn't even a special needs situation, yet. It was basic.

"Is there something you need help saying to the teacher?" Or that Mommy can help translate?

"May I please go to the bathroom?" He offered. *Right.*

No kid should have to put up with this crap. I had to find a way to get him help in the classroom that couldn't be ignored.

I made an appointment with the school principal. It was time to see what Steven was doing for myself. I wanted to perform an observation—a small request, in my opinion. I'd just sit unobtrusively in the back of the room with a notepad. Mrs. Edward wasn't on board. I think I made her a little uncomfortable with the request.

It was *I* who would be watched, however. The push to find out what we could do to help this boy resulted in a mini-legal battle. Did I mention, as foster parents, we also had no legal rights to manage his education? That would've been nice to know before I did what I did. I had to learn the hard way.

The school combed through Steven's records. Not only did they make it abundantly clear to me that I had no rights to his education, including the request for special needs accommodations, I was also not permitted on the school campus. His biological family still held the legal rights to his education and all the privileges that come with it. I was escorted off the premise.

Ryan was also blacklisted. He went to the school office with a form of sorts to be filled out. It shouldn't have been a big deal. He introduced himself to the office admin as Steven's father, Ryan Molony. They looked at the form and back up at him.

"You mean, foster parent?"

Ryan corrected them. "No. I'm his dad."

"Yeah, but, not really." *Woah.* Something had to be done about this.

Gaining limited guardianship rights to manage Steven's educational plan and medical care was something we had to get cleared through the courts. Request after request was sent to Steven's social worker, Susan. I forwarded the school's correspondences and begged for help. Anything providing justification for our request was sent to Susan. This included the e-mail exchange from the day Steven was assaulted at school.

My e-mail read:

> *"Dear Mrs. Edwards, Steven reported to us today that he received a bloody nose when a fellow classmate named Daniel punched him, then walked away. He says it happened at the first recess, before lunch. He said he told you about it then did not go to the nurse. He washed himself off in a drinking fountain. He had bled so much, it was splattered over the front of his uniform. Can you please tell us more? We need to submit an incident report to his social worker within 24 hours. Thanks!"*

Defensive Debbie Edward responded as follows:

> *"Steven notified me about this at the end of the day. He did not elaborate on how he got the bloody nose and he was not bleeding at that time. He said he got the bloody nose at recess but did not specify which recess. It sounds like the incident was handled and no further action was needed."*

Thanks for your e-mails, Mrs. Edward. *That* specific record wound up in court. Proving our child was in more harm outside of our authority than in was exactly what we needed. Susan successfully petitioned to terminate the biological mother's legal rights to Steven's education and medical care... so *we* could have it. *Finally.*

The legal limitations on foster parents to access this important information is understandable—to a point. I can respect when a foster child is supposed to be returning to their biological parents for reunification, this step to transfer guardianship back and forth might be a bit too much. But when we're talking about long-term care, no reunification in sight, or when obvious special medical attention is required... things should be different.

If I was temporarily unavailable to parent my child, I don't think it would be necessary for a surrogate parent to have my child's *entire* history of medical records and authorization for major treatments. That being said, I would strongly agree with making sure they knew as much as possible in order to ensure my baby was well cared for.

In the future, would it be too much to ask for biological parents or other family members to complete a survey with basic facts so the foster families could even have a starting point? A reasonable disclosure of sorts:

> *Here's her medication. This is the pediatrician's number, if you have any problems. She likes to sleep on her back. She's a fussy eater.*

Babysitters get more information than we did!

Now, if I could truly change the world of foster care, I would also ask for a survey of recent stressors that might impact the child's stay with another family. *Any exposure to drug use? Accidents or deaths? Fires? Domestic violence?*

For the benefit of my child, I would reveal the answers. I would want them to get the best care possible until I could return. And I definitely I wouldn't want the family they stayed with to struggle with, fear, or resent my child.

Misty reminded me about the importance of acceptance. "The System" (the foster care system, the educational system, and so on) could not be changed just for me. The past could not be changed for him. The healing process could not be sped up. And some answers would never come.

She called this an "opportunity" for me.

The medical files we received were sparse, but I took nothing for granted. Full-term baby. Teen mom: smoker, addict. Several times in his infancy, he was admitted to the emergency room with severe medical concerns. My heart pounded as I read and re-read every page for clues. *I found one.*

"He has a weak cry," the page read. "He has no tears." It was an odd comment for the circumstances of that particular visit. Suspicious, for sure. A baby that doesn't cry, even when sick, in fear or in pain. *Imagine that.*

This didn't sit well with me. We had learned in our foster parent training about the cycle of attachment. This is how babies learn to get their needs met when in distress. They cry, the caretaker meets the need, then the child is soothed. This process, repeated hundreds or thousands of times while the child's brain is developing, establishes neurological pathways critical for emotional regulation and the formation of healthy relationships. Essentially, the baby learns how to communicate a need and *who* to trust to meet it.

Unfortunately, when children do not have their needs met, they can develop an insecure attachment to the caretaker, or remain unattached. And unable to trust.

I remembered a guest speaker in our foster care training describing a visit to an orphanage in Russia.

"It's silent," they said. "The babies there don't cry because they've learned when they cry, no one comes."

This doesn't mean they don't have a need. They *remain* in distress, in pain, and in misery… but in silence.

I tracked Steven's height and weight and found that he didn't grow for two years. *Why?*

The day we met him, I remember Susan going over the basic information with us. When she revealed that he was seven, I had to do a double-take. Steven was tiny. By "tiny," I mean he was wearing size 4T toddler clothes.

We can implicate stress as one cause for stunted growth, but we would also find out from Steven that, for a while, he went without food. His story just kept getting worse!

"What do you mean you didn't eat?" I asked him.

"I begged for food," Steven explained. "If we didn't have enough, I gave my food to my sister." *Wow.* That was rather mature for a three or four-year-old.

I tried to understand. "Begged? What?! Who did you beg from?"

"Everyone. My teachers. People outside. Sometimes the neighbor gave us milk."

My heart ached. Call it ignorance, or "a strong sense of justice," but I believed this kind of thing wasn't supposed to happen to children. And definitely not in America.

Teachers are supposed to be mandated reporters of abuse and neglect. The neighbors should have seen a pattern. They were *guilty* in my mind. They knew! *Why was the starvation and neglect allowed to continue?*

I'm certain that if a child ever begged me for food, I would have raised some red flags, made some calls, and figured out what the *hell* was going on. And I would have fed that child.

But I wasn't there. *I wasn't there for Steven when he needed food.* I'd have to forgive myself for that.

"Where was your mom?" I pushed.

Steven winced. I hit a nerve and instantly regretted it.

He looked away and sighed, "I don't know."

Chapter 9

Seeing Past The Paperwork

Armed with our new guardianship rights, we spent months taking Steven to a mind-boggling amount of doctor's appointments. To be specific, in the first six months with us, he averaged twenty-three appointments per month. *You can add them up.*

I may have overreacted by taking Steven *everywhere* I could think of to find the answers we sought. Maybe I just needed to relax. Maybe I should have let time tell me all. Could *one* professional opinion be enough? It felt like we were only getting "best guesses" from people with a minimal investment in my child's life. We were temporary and symptomatic.

But I needed more than the school's IEP and pills for a relationship with Steven to work. I needed hope. And so did he! After all, I wasn't the only person in the room hearing constant bad news about him. It was muddling up the story, and Steven was *already* dealing with a junior identity crisis.

So, I made my way through the traditional practitioners, therapists, and every Biblical reference I could lay my hands on. I knew that somewhere in the narrative, we'd find a through-line truth.

After being put on a long wait list, we finally got in to see the local psychologist. It took several weeks to get an appointment at the *only* clinic in our city that accepted the state's insurance program for foster youth. I had one shot to make this work.

All my notes were ready. E-mails from his school teacher, patterns of behaviors, journal entries, and stories Steven had been telling us about his past. This was something I had become good at—being prepared for investigations and getting results.

At one time, I was the operations manager and an expert consultant for a safety and compliance organization. I got paid to make companies accident-proof and blame-resistant. I could recite occupational safety manuals as easily as the Bible. I believed I knew the laws and regulations better than the lawyers and regulators did. And I was good at my job. Irreplaceable.

One of my favorite and most hated tasks was to investigate a workplace "accident." It might be an injury, destruction of property, or even a death. As much as I'd love to claim that I solved every investigation like Jessica Chastain's character in *Zero Dark Thirty,* it was a bit more like using Jedi mind-tricks to dissuade authorities from bringing heat to my clients. Truth, data and other evidence, when presented in a curated sequence, could lead investigators and claimants to the exact conclusion I wanted them to have. Every problem had a solution.

But at home, I felt absolutely clueless trying to piece together Steven's past life. Years later, I would find peace on this matter. But right then, I was getting rather frustrated when all the answers painted a picture only as clear as a Pollock painting.[16] They were answers *without* answers.

I collected a list of suspected life events that might have caused the external manifestations of health, appearance, and behaviors we saw in Steven. I was hunting down a cause, or as I called it at work, "the antecedent." I just never imagined that the answer could be "all of the above."

The psychologist was chubby and weather-worn. I thought I was pretty good at handling horror-story tales of terrible events in people's lives. It made my job easier. *This woman, however...*

She appeared to feel a sense of loss as I spoke. She kept stressing how sorry she was—for us, or him—and how hard this situation was.

I didn't need her to be sorry for me.

We had come into the psychologist's office for a full intake and establishment of a treatment plan. I wanted solutions, not pity.

After a long discussion, several surveys, a historical information disclosure, and time alone with Steven, the assessment was complete. The psychologist could sum up and come up with a clear path toward recovery. She wasn't as optimistic as I was, however.

16 Jackson Pollock was an abstract painter in America (1912-1956). He was well known for flicking or flinging paint from the end of the paintbrush to land seemingly "anywhere" on the canvas. Though this required planning and effort, the resulting canvas had no distinct image for a viewer to glean meaning from.

Though the reports would take time to finish, she did have a few choice words to leave me with.

"You are so brave," she commented. *Me? How so?* "...For trying to stick this out."

She asked how long he would be staying with us. I thought she needed to know in order to adjust the treatment plan accordingly. Maybe she'd worked with foster families in the past and knew how to accommodate?

"Forever," I threw out. Perhaps, I meant to say, "long-term," or something less serious. Perhaps, I didn't. Ask Freud. As far as I knew, no one else was coming along to get Steven. Ryan and I were determined to do what was right for the boy.

She nodded thoughtfully, then added, "So you think."

The results in the psychological report were crushing, but not in the way most people would think. Yes, I had to wrap my mind around some strong emotions, including fear and sadness. But the real blow was a logistical mess. On one hand, we could now get this boy into helpful programs and begin therapy because we had a strong case for it.

On the other hand, the information it included would have unintended consequences at our adoption application signing. Apparently, there are some points of no return in the mental health category. We would soon face the challenge of adopting the "un-adoptable."

In Steven's report, there was a section with variables titled "Mental Status." It indicated impairments and the severities of each. It ran the gamut of simple inattentiveness all the way to homicidal thoughts. Half of the boxes were flagged as an impairment. *Woah.* I don't mean they were "possibilities." They were marked as "truths."

The psychologist labeled his dysfunctional thoughts and erratic violence accordingly.

The next section read "Functional Impairment." This reviewed day-to-day functions and one's capacity to perform them. Items included were bathing, toileting, and feeding. Sixty percent of these items were flagged. *Sounds about right.*

The notes about Steven's condition identified him as a threat to other children. It read, "This is a lifetime illness." She told me I would have to come to terms with it.

I told *her* to jump off a cliff.

Just kidding. I only thought about it.

Instead, I asked, "How soon can we start the treatments?"

I understand the report created a lot of concerns. That was a hefty psychosis diagnosis for him! But I didn't realize at the time what it would mean for *me*. It simply didn't register.

Even if it did, the diagnoses didn't matter more than the child did. Steven wasn't going anywhere. Ryan loved him already. I was trying. And since he is the only child we'd ever raised, we had no point of reference for how our different our lives would or could have been any different. All of his quirks were "normal" to us. This was just the way it was.

Of course, I wasn't naïve. I knew his actions were not acceptable by society. The violence was and is scary. The lack of boundaries and remorse, or understanding of cause and effect made living with Steven risky.

I had to make a choice of what to believe. Would this boy's past forever define his future, like the doctor was suggesting? Or, was healing possible? Could he ever overcome the deficits his biological family left him with?

My faith was being challenged. In the Bible, faith is defined as the "confident assurance that something we want is going to happen. It is the certainty that what we hope for is waiting for us, even though we cannot see it up ahead."[17] I might expand on this with, "even if no one else around you can see it *either*."

My faith taught me to believe that all things are possible with the help of God.[18] He gives us the strength we need to overcome—including healing and radical changes of the heart. Although Steven was not yet who I dreamed "my son" would be, I had to know that there was more to this boy than his past. I had to believe he had a future.

Let me be clear on this point: I wasn't preparing to become this boy's savior. The plan was never to "rescue" anyone through adoption. But I knew someone who *could* redeem my son from his past and give him hope for his future.[19]

I looked online for a spiritual healer. There were more options than I was prepared for. Who could I trust with such a delicate situation? Who could give me insights beyond what a physical exam could produce?

My church pastors would cringe if they found out we went to a psychic.

---

17 Hebrews, Chapter 11, verse 1. The Living Bible translation.

18 1. "Looking at them, Jesus said, 'With people it is impossible, but not with God; for all things are possible with God.'" (Mark 10:27, New American Standard)
2. "For I can do everything through Christ, who gives me strength." (Philippians 4:13, New Living Translation)

19 Jeremiah 29:11 ****xi.***

"Well, I don't usually work with children this young," the healer told me. I don't remember her name, but it seems fitting to call her Genie. She looked the part.

"Why?" I had explained the situation on the phone before making the appointment. She smiled warmly. Her whole body exuded warmth, really.

"They don't follow directions as well as adults." *Ah-ha!* That, I understood well.

For today's hypnosis session, Steven would sit in the room and listen to the story I would tell, ie. "channel his energy into it." I would take a hypno-nap and try not to roll my closed eyes. I was extremely skeptical.

"Let's begin." Genie relaxed back onto her chair with a notepad in hand. "Take a few breaths. Good. Now, I want you to imagine you're taking a walk." *Where?*

"Can you tell me where you are?" *Huh? No. Was I supposed to make it up?*

"Just look around. When you are ready, describe what you see." *Ohmygosh. She was reading my mind!*

"Out loud, please." *Oh, oops! No, she wasn't. I knew that.*

The whole process was a series of bizarre requests to wander around in my imagination, climb staircases that went nowhere in particular, pick up objects that mysteriously appeared on the ground, and respond to a person who was talking to me just outside of my view.

I'll admit a good portion of the time involved thinking, "What if I *don't* go up the stairs, but dug a hole and climbed down into it instead? How much does she get paid per minute?" And, of course, "Don't fart."

As much as I enjoy the satire, there was actually a story that came from the experience—one that would confuse me for years, but a story, nonetheless.

I found Steven alone on the beach. He was crouched low, toddleresque, playing in the sand, talking to no one. I couldn't hear his voice. No one could. I approached him, but he never let me touch him. He didn't seem afraid—just untouchable. He reminded me of a forest sprite of sorts. Not quite feral.

I tried asking him some questions and he responded, but still, no sound was produced. Lying on the chaise, my eyes welled up with tears. *Why couldn't I understand him?* I realized that my vision was not "whatever" I wanted it to be. I *wanted* him to be able to talk to me. And trust me.

Steven walked off towards a tree line and I followed.

"Where is he going?" *Were those my thoughts or Genie's?*

Steven kept leading me into a quiet forest. It was a little like playing hide-and-seek. Finally, he came to a stop near no tree in particular. He wanted to show me something. Steven dug through the forest floor at the base of the tree. He unearthed leaves, moss, and soil to reveal a box buried below. *Now what?*

"What's in the box?" Genie assumed I could open it, therefore, I could. *Abracadabra!* Oh, the box contained a heart. *How cliché.*

I tried to pick up the heart, but Steven yanked the box back from my hands, slammed the lid, and snarled. *What the heck, Dobby?!*

The Elven vagrant furiously re-buried his treasure. I was allowed to know where it was buried, but I could not have it. Those were the rules.

Opening my eyes, I asked, "What was the point of that?" We ended the session.

Genie nodded along with her gentle "Hmm."

"Do you know what the heart represented?" She prompted. Was the meaning of this up to me?

Then again, I knew. It was love for a mother.

Initially, I considered the visit to the psychic a waste of time. It took a couple of years to make any sense.

My son and I were neck deep in attachment therapy. Sometimes it's called "Thera-play." We were breaking down residual barriers preventing us from connecting to each other years after the adoption.

Steven had assigned me the title of "Mother," but it was somewhat artificial—heavy on function, lite on emotion. In other words, I had access to the box, but still couldn't have what was inside. He held many parts of himself in reserve. Physical touch was still an issue. Trust was still an issue. Anger was a constant.

One night over dinner, Steven shared his thoughts on how the therapy sessions were going. His fork idled over the plate, uncertain of where it might land.

"It's hard," he frowned. "I love going with you… but then we come home and I feel sad." His brows scrunched as he looked up at us. Ryan and I shared a glance.

"Hmm… What do you think is making you sad?" I offered. His face fell back to his plate as he spoke.

"My mom broke my heart. So, I broke yours, too."

I know, Baby. I know.

In my desperation, I scheduled one more special appointment. This time, I found something called a "Healing Room." A Bible-based ministry trained people at this location to develop their prayer lives and attunement to God's voice. For some readers, this might sound crazier than my trip to the psychic. That's fair.

The folks that worked there practiced praying with people for miraculous healing. Some prophesied (revealed the future). Others had the ability to discern the needs of an individual and speak to the root of their problem to provide guidance (like a mind reader). Though I had known about skills such as these from being raised in a church, I did not have much experience with *this* kind of thing.

"Can I bring in my child?" I asked the receptionist. It would be a long drive to get there and we would be home late, past Steven's bedtime.

This school of sorts was set up like a doctor's office. The receptionist handed me a clipboard with forms and questionnaires. After a short lobby wait, we were called back into a small room and introduced to two women. One was the "trainer/mentor," the other was a "student."

I proceeded to explain all the difficulties of our lives at this point. Looking ahead at a lifetime of medical appointments, pills, therapies, and the possibility that none of it would even work left me feeling hopeless, confused, and tired. We also went over Steven's concerns.

The women were extraordinarily patient and listened to us without comment or concern. This was exactly the type of response I was hoping for from the psychologist! No one should be treated by a physician that is more openly worried than they are. Those who are well-informed and have solutions to problems, whether physical, mental, or spiritual, should be calmer than the suffering patient, notwithstanding. *Can I have an Amen?*

The women asked for a moment of silence to pray for understanding.[20]

---

20 "Trust in the Lord with all your heart and lean not on your own understanding; in

Steven's response came first. There was an army of soldiers assembling. An anointing on his life requires him to prepare for an upcoming battle. Nothing that has happened in Steven's past will derail the plan God has for him. He has been fortified.

This message was one shade lighter than the psychic meditation. "Fortified" is the opposite of "broken." *Lord, help me to see what You see.*

My answers came next. I was a weapons maker. I was to build the sharpest, strongest, most effective tools for Steven. I could not go to battle with or for him, but I *could* equip him with the exact armaments he needed and teach him how to use them well. None of the work would be in vain. No time would be wasted. No loss would go unredeemed.

As cool as that all sounds, I had to wrap my head around three very different pictures of what life with Steven would look like. Was it a life sentence or a ministry to his broken heart? Or, was there something greater? Believing there was something bigger happening in this situation sealed the deal for me. It provided the ability to hope and dream for this child.

In this soul-search, I determined Steven's health was worth the effort it would require to be restored. I also held on to the idea that I have (and always had) what it would take to help him be successful.

This didn't make things easier in a practical sense, however. We'd *barely* come close to the six-month mark in our relationship. Who knew what else might come up if we took the plunge to adopt

all your ways submit to Him and he will make your path straight." (Proverbs 3:5-6, New International Version)

Steven? Selfishly, I was afraid of what it might cost me in terms of my time and energy, career status, and social identity.

You adopted a boy you barely knew? A boy with that kind of past? With those disorders?! Yes. It would shock some people.

I had to figure out if I could be afraid and still maintain faith in the assurances I now clung to. Could faith and fear co-exist? I believe they did. At least, at the *beginning* of the journey.

At that point, I was struggling with giving up pre-programmed expectations, good and bad, for this boy and myself.[21] I had to learn to trust in God while I was still on the journey – not just when I arrived at my destination.[22]

21 "There is no fear in love, but perfect love drives out fear, because fear has punishment; and the one fearing has not been perfected in love." (1st John 4:18, Berean Literal Bible)

22 "For we walk by faith, not by sight." (2nd Corinthians 5:7, New Living Translation)

Chapter 10

Be Careful What You Wish For

We were at the six-month point. Steven had been living with us as a foster youth with no positive action being taken from his biological family to reunify. This meant two things: 1. His parents would have their legal ability to claim Steven permanently severed. 2. Steven's social worker, Susan, would write a proposal to the Family Court judge for a permanent placement and/or adoption arrangement. Steven needed a forever home—*now*. It could either be us, or someone else.

Children's Welfare set a meeting to include Ryan and me, a representative from our adoption agency, and Susan. A critical objective for this meeting was to update Steven's foster youth profile with the state. For us, it was also a chance to show our interest and readiness to adopt.

To prepare, we gathered all existing records of services Steven had been receiving. We needed evidence of medical diagnoses, school performance, and therapy progress notes. I collected as many receipts as possible to show the expenses incurred regarding mileage and fees paid towards medical care. The state would use the severity of medical concerns to set a caretaker stipend rate. It was like filing taxes, but an accounting of *human* value, if you will.

The items collected created a portfolio the judge could use to assess what type of ongoing care Steven would need from his future family. This was all standard operating procedure, regardless of the outcome. We hoped Susan would use the documents as evidence at the hearing to qualify us as an appropriate choice for an adoptive family. Still, there was no guarantee the judge would choose us on the basis of longevity alone.

"Get a babysitter," the agency recommended, rather businesslike. "You will not want Steven to hear anything said at this meeting."

We held the meeting at home around our kitchen table. Each person brought their briefcase, notepads, and file folders along. I prepared iced tea while catching up with Misty. Ryan chose the seat nearest to an exit. He'd always been somewhat allergic to paperwork.

Before we began, someone from the state visited with Steven in the living room. They would observe him in our home, then briefly take him out of earshot, feed him candy, and ask veiled questions about his well-being. The latter served as one way to make sure foster children are not being abused by the families they stayed with. *Good.*

The babysitter was ready and waiting for their park date.

"Try to keep him out for at least an hour. Maybe two," I instructed the teen. Steven would be fine. She was the most responsible fifteen-year-old I'd ever met—a sweet homeschooled daughter of a mom-friend. As I checked the backpack one more time for sunblock and water bottles, Mr. Wells, the director of the adoption agency, finished flipping through the portfolio I laid out. Ryan shifted in his seat and the small talk ended.

"Are these *all* the medical reports?" Mr. Wells looked over at me.

"Uh-huh."

"I see we're looking at an autism diagnosis." *Yeah? So?* "The trauma history and other behaviors can improve. There are many therapies that can help." Smiling, he offered, "And you are doing a great job with finding them." A compliment before a critique.

"But with autism," he took a breath. "Well, there are just some things that will *never* improve."

Mr. Wells watched carefully for my reaction. I don't know what he wanted from me. Was he waiting for me to break down? Be shocked? To cry? He must have been expecting something other parents have done. But he wouldn't get that response from either of us.

Ryan and I both suspected Steven was on the spectrum within the first few days of meeting him. These reports did not surprise us in the least. As his parents—foster parents—we *knew,* and we understood what kind of help he needed. His deficits were clear as day. We targeted his therapies and were already doing everything we could at home to adapt to his rhythm. By this time, we had come to a place of acceptance far beyond what we had initially imagined. We were "all-in."

Also, we quickly figured Susan's initial report to the agency of "no medical concerns" for this boy was far from true. It may have been "carefully curated," as I would say.

This made me wonder. Perhaps the people Steven stayed with previously had ensured this lack of medical documentation as a means to an end?

But none of that mattered now.

We read through the remaining documents as a group, including the incident reports from Steven's more violent days. Susan sorted pages into various paperclips and added sticky notes as we finished discussing the psychologist's findings.

Mr. Wells grunted. "This is heavy stuff." The kitchen chair squeaked underneath him in reply.

"Are you considering moving forward with an adoption petition?"

My heart skipped a beat. "Yes, we would like to be considered."

Ryan squeezed my hand under the table. He locked eyes with Mr. Wells and nodded his agreement.

Ever the realist, Mr. Wells reminded us how we had initially applied for multiple children. We expressed a desire to grow the family with siblings—either all at once or over time. This ambition remains in our hearts today.

When he spoke next, it was "as a concerned friend." The guise would help shed light on a major conflict of interest regarding Steven's future with us.

"All things considered, under these circumstances, you will probably never be placed with a child again." This announcement haunts me more than any threat Steven has ever uttered.

I had to take a moment to replay this news in my head in order to hear it clearly. *I'll never carry my own child. This is the only one I've had a chance with. And now, you're saying I won't have another? Ever?*

Discoveries regarding Steven's mental health and safety officially classified him as a threat to other children. The state even considered it a dangerous situation for the expectant parents. Finally, Steven's profile with the state would change in such a way to cause him to become virtually unadoptable.

I didn't know if Mr. Wells was *for* us or *against* us anymore. Misty stayed quiet.

"If we had known the extent of his, er… 'situation,' we never would have placed him in your home." Was Mr. Wells… apologizing? At this, the color drained from Ryan's face, but the blood inside *my* body heated up.

Glances shot around the table. Another eye-conversation transpired between the agency director and the state social worker, Susan.

Susan looked sorry for us. She would have a very hard time finding a family to care for him if we did not proceed with an adoption. "It's possible. There are group homes… certain therapeutic placements… residency programs…"

They were formulating an exit strategy!

I felt nauseated. What did I just do? I hadn't expected my over-achieving to backfire like this. Finding out what was wrong with Steven might cost him his future and risk ours. And it was all my fault for finding out so much about him!

Something in me snapped.

I wasn't mad about the legalities. I wasn't mad at Steven. I wasn't even mad about the other children we might never have. I was mad because *these people* put me in charge of a boy who was lost in the system: health neglected, education ignored, and abandoned by everyone else in his life. But me? I fought for Steven. I had gone through hell to get him the care and treatments he deserved.

Mr. Wells' words stung like a backhanded slap. After all I'd done. After all we'd been through! Ryan and I demonstrated more competency and adaptability than words can describe. We were *not* the same people who filled out an application two years before. Parenting changed us. Steven changed us.

"It might be wise to take a few days to think about this before you make a..."

"No!" Ryan interjected. "We're okay. This doesn't scare us. He's ours."

Ryan's words spoke volumes more than mine. The agency director overtly doubted his ability to parent from the beginning. He greatly underestimated us.

Mr. Wells turned to me. "Are *you* still sure you want to move forward?"

I could have been one of the last people they expected to stand up for Steven. But with a final glance to Ryan, I became a mom.

"Where do I sign?"

Ryan and I weren't people to give up easily. We were fighters. It's why we had been successful in our careers. This wasn't the first or last time we'd face a turning point in our lives. It was also not the first time we had gone head-to-head with the wonderfully accepting and understanding adoption agency I found.

The agency director made his disapproval known right after we began working with them. After two months in foster parent training and the long-awaited completion of our home study, we were finally browsing through children's profiles. While *we* thought were on the road to parenthood back then, something was eating at Mr. Wells.

He called us in for a formal meeting. Mr. Wells insisted it would have to be held at the agency's location two hours away—in person.

"We have some concerns about moving forward." Mr. Wells' terseness drove me crazy.

"What does that mean?" I asked, crossing my legs and leaning back into Ryan's side. I tried to look comfortable even if I didn't feel the part. That day, the agency expressed concern about our marriage being a bit "uneven." My enthusiasm far outweighed Ryan's, and they weren't certain of his overall investment in the adoption.

Mr. Wells outlined Ryan's crimes from the agency's viewpoint. "You didn't participate in the discussion activities during training. It appears you haven't filled out a single form on your own. And I have a quote from your initial interview that says, 'No one really knows how to be a parent before kids. I'll just figure it out as I go along.'" And that, folks, is *exactly* what Ryan did.

Knowing these sticking points, spouses, make sure you *both* fill out your application forms in your own handwriting with different colored pens. Why? So both of you can suffer through the paperwork equally!

I digress.

Our application was suspended. Mr. Wells gave us a six-month "no contact" arrangement, after which we could show an "improved" marital relationship or close the account. We drove four hours, round-trip, to hear that.

We began marriage counseling shortly after. That's what happens when someone sticks a wedge between couples.

Six months later, we presented Mr. Wells with a note from our church pastor showing we had completed a series of counseling sessions. We were invited back on one condition: we would have to complete foster parent training *all over again* with Ryan under the microscope.

Throughout our foster-to-adoption journey, Ryan and I had strong support from our parents and fellow church members who encouraged us before this was a reality. The foster parent community provided wonderful connections to others who understood us and made us feel "at home" in our little world. But we also faced many doubters. Plenty of negative comments came from people whose opinions didn't matter. Those were easy to brush off. But there were a few extra hard-to-hear doubts from people whose opinions mattered greatly—like close friends and family.

My youngest sister put it like this: "You don't know what you're doing." She was right, in a way. But what first-time parent does? It hurt for someone who has known me all my life to have absolutely no confidence in me.

Then my brother joined the club. We wanted to designate him as a Godparent, should Ryan and I die. Upon receiving an abbreviated disclosure of our son's past, present, and future medical needs, he opted out. It was a gut-blow I didn't see coming. To make a long story short, he told me, "I love you… but I can't do that." Clenching my teeth, I wrote his name on a form, anyway. At the time, we had no other options and assigning guardianship was a requirement for the adoption petition.

The point I'm trying to make is that just because *you* believe you have what it takes, does not mean that the people nearest to you will automatically or unconditionally join you on this path. You will need to adjust your relationship expectations.

The adoption agency we were *paying* constantly thwarted us. Cherished friends from church cut off our relationship in order to "protect" their own children from the child we now housed. Even my closest childhood friend criticized me for writing my story.

"You asked for this," she said. "Don't act like you didn't."

Chapter 11

This Is Uncomfortable

I didn't ask for a child with a dark past. Nor did I ask for a child with life-altering mental illnesses. And, no, I didn't ask for my community to fall apart, for my identity to be shifted, or for my child to suffer criticism everywhere we went. That's why we set parameters at the beginning of this journey. But God had other plans, it seemed.

His plans were bigger than Steven's circumstantial placement with us. They were bigger than the adoption. They are bigger still than the impact of this book. God's wisdom is greater than ours and He knows there is more to our stories than the page we are currently on.[23]

---

23 "Let us fix our eyes on Jesus, the author and perfecter of our faith, who for the joy set before Him endured the cross, scorning its shame, and sat down at the right hand of the throne of God." (Hebrews 12:2, Berean Study Bible)

Ryan and I were just beginning a new chapter, complete with twists and turns.[24]

How *does* a foster youth with a rap sheet get presented to a family with "no (known) medical concerns?" I have my theories, but no proof.

When a child has problems, misses important milestones, or acts out, *no one* does anything about it. The formula is simple: no doctor visits means there is no paperwork, and no paper trail means there is no traceable medical problem.

Remember, foster parents typically have very little influence over medical treatments for their youth. Some people feel strongly that *only* biological parents, not the foster-babysitters, should manage or decide on long-term, or more serious medical procedures. It would not behoove someone with a temporary parental mindset to increase the medical attention they need to provide for a child in their care. If this happens, the family will be stuck maintaining the level of care—as I was. Whatever the doctor recommends or prescribes the foster parent absolutely must do.

More prescriptions result in more medication management—which also means more paperwork for the state. More questions for the doctor could cause more referrals, which leads to more appointments, more expenses, and so on. Last, more diagnoses

24 "In all things, God works for the good of those who love him…" (Romans 8:28, New International Version)

could increase the challenge of moving, or in our case *keeping*, a child placed under your care.

On the flip-side, more intense medical attention and certain "severe" diagnoses can result in higher caretaker stipends. With Steven's new bill of health, the rate assessed after the recent meeting increased by $1,000 per month. *Dang*.

After the adoption, there is absolutely zero accounting for what you, the adoptive parent, spend that money on. New kitchen cabinets, anyone? How about a vacation? It does sound appealing. Now, factor in these deductions:

- The child you have must be under constant supervision because he's a security threat. You work 24-hours per day. In shifts, if you are lucky.
- The child's dramatic learning challenges require you to set aside your income-earning job and begin homeschooling.
- Medical appointments are so frequent that your monthly gasoline bill triples or quadruples. Say goodbye to afternoon play dates. You'll be busy!
- Vehicle and property damage become a daily occurrence. Insurance rates go up.
- Parental anxiety, depression, and social isolation add more health, marital, and financial problems to the mix.

With only five types of expenses listed so far, and even with the stipend, my "income" dropped below the 2015 poverty level, as reported by the Office of the Federal Register. *Dang, again.*

Another theory of mine is many children in foster care change placements frequently enough to create a massive disconnect in their ongoing medical care—regardless of what is prescribed.

From one house to another, it can be difficult to follow through with a treatment plan effectively. It's unfair, but the children can get stuck labeled as "bad" or a misfit, defiant, or aggressive because they don't have the resources to be seen as anything else. These children need an advocate to stand up for them—setting aside all pre-conceived notions and believing there is more to them than their past. Or their paperwork.

Now that Ryan and I were officially "family planning," we would have to take a closer look at the kind of life we wanted to offer Steven. Our thickened skins were frequently being chafed, as it was.

We got looks.

"Is his father… *dark*?" This was asked of me while on a school field trip. A woman in a purple blouse stared at Steven and me from across the aisle of the bus.

"Nope. He's White," I replied. I looked her straight in the eye and smiled, daring her to continue. Very few people even knew what to ask next. The mention of him having two moms or two dads also raised eyebrows.

Depending on how bold I felt in these awkward exchanges regarding my child's bi-racialness, I sometimes played along and said something like, "Oh, well… You know… Ryan's not *actually* the father." A good, hard wink sealed that note.

We were criticized.

"He didn't get *anything* correct on his test today," Mrs. Edwards complained. That would affect her classroom score. She handed over a folder stuffed with Steven's week of assignments. It looked like he hadn't completed much work, but he had some nice doodles of animals, spirals, blobs and such. I half-expected a pink slip for the doodles.

"I thought you were working on these concepts with him at home," the teacher spat at me. I was. It was a battle, but I could find ways to help him focus and complete the work she sent. He just wouldn't do it in class.

We were avoided.

One Sunday at church, Steven complained about the loud music in his kids' class. I brought him in with me to the main service, but he went into sensory overload there, too. A rapid decline in his mental facilities resulted in Steven regressing to babbling and needing to be rocked like a baby to soothe him. He wasn't loud, but it was obvious to those around us. The woman sitting to our left whispered an "Excuse me," got up and walked away. Steven accidentally bumped the chair in front of us. A cute, young couple shared a less quiet he-said-she-said.

"I can't deal with this."

"Let's find somewhere else to sit."

Things changed when we claimed Steven as ours. Folks seemed more lenient when the family situation was considered impermanent—especially the school.

I suppose it's easy to be welcoming and patient with a child who was challenging once or twice, but thrice was too much of a burden. And long-term? I guess I couldn't blame them. We all have our own maximum tolerance for stress.

Ryan's father once told me that I had "the patience of Job," a relentlessly tormented character from the Bible who never gave up hope. It appeared so, but this wasn't true. I put up with a lot from Steven, but I couldn't continue being surrounded by constant negativity from everyone else.

As a result of the discomfort, we left our church, we arranged our finances so I could stop working, and we withdrew Steven from his school. I was doing all the work with him at home anyway. How different could homeschooling be?

Steven's anxiety in a traditional school classroom never eased. The IEP evaluations shook loose a grocery list of problems we were up against: dyslexia, dysgraphia, visual processing disorder, language processing disorder, sensory processing disorder… and of course, the co-morbid autism and ADHD. The disorder concoction was simply too much for the educators to address.

Steven made no academic progress during his attendance, even with remedial lessons from a special education teacher. This was unacceptable. Fed up with being ostracized by the teacher's critical attitude towards us, we pulled the plug on the school.

With the support of my homeschooling mom-friend, I was able to get plugged in to a group of families who had been teaching at home for years. They held a wealth of knowledge and experience for me to draw from. They were also incredibly accepting of my future son. Several families were raising children with special needs of their own. Some had also adopted. Many were Christian families who, over time, impressed upon me the incalculable value of an individualized education in a home setting. The child's heart was to be engaged as much as their mind.

I enjoyed homeschooling as a practice, but also as a culture and mindset. It empowered our family to be more responsive to Steven's needs. I could use curricula tailored toward children with learning differences. We became free to pursue more intensive therapies because our weekly schedule was now wide open. We made long-lasting friendships with other like-minded families. Steven and I even tagged along on Ryan's work trips to other cities and snuck in whatever sights we could see as "educational field trips." It was one of the best decisions we have ever made regarding our overall family health. But it wasn't easy. Steven still had his bad days.

Away from the social restrictions of the classroom environment, Steven entertained his inner demons more. Instead of stewing in dysfunctional thoughts at school, then exploding when he got home, Steven could let out a steady stream of anger throughout his day. The pending adoption plan was a two-sided coin for him. Finding a forever family simultaneously emphasized the finality of abandonment by his first family. He needed time and space to grieve.

Besides the emotional turmoil bubbling over, I began taking on a full day's dose of the "-oses." Steven's hyperactivity was *so* much worse than I had remembered from the summer we met. Essential oils and vitamin supplements were not doing the trick. We were both hemorrhaging brain power.

I slowly began to believe I was not doing a "good enough" job of providing solutions for Steven's problems. My self-esteem took a hit. But on a more positive note, we were almost fully potty-trained and he was sleeping through the night!

Chapter 12

The Most Special School, Ever

Steven loved the idea that every day was "pajama day" as a home-schooler. Though I relaxed on many of the typical school constructs, I did try to keep his days highly organized. Lessons were supposed to be from 8:00 am to 12:00 pm. Because we worked one-on-one, he completed activities quickly with no distractions or delays typically found in a class full of students. He made progress faster than I'd expected.

The exception to this was in reading and writing. What we didn't know at the time was that the visual perception dysfunctions were impeding his brain's ability to even register most symbols on the page *as* symbols. Letters might as well have been chicken scratch, flashes of light, or even upside-down and floating off the page. This held him back from being able to read the cool dinosaur fact book we got from the library.

If we had known, we would have begun pediatric vision therapy sooner. Our traditional medical insurance didn't cover this, though, and it ran up an out of pocket bill of nearly $7,000. Thank God for those stipends.

That being said: it's worth the year-long commitment and expense. Improving his eyesight would affect his reading, coordination, balance, and more. It would raise his confidence.

Reading time crushed Steven. If I read to him, he understood. If he had to read, it was a disaster.

"Let's work on some reading and writing," I announced. Steven yanked the book from my fingers and flung it down the hallway, ripping a page out in the process. The alphabet poster had recently been shredded as well. Like I said, it was a battle.

"You can't make me read," He snarled. "I read *yesterday*! I'm sick of reading!"

"Steven, what the...?" I didn't even have a chance to finish. Hot tears overflowed from his eyes. The same book which had frustrated him a day ago was now a loose page dropping from a fist. With both hands, he pulled at the skin on his face. His eyelids stretched as he growled in anguish. His "stupid" eyes couldn't read the letters.

"No! You don't have to do this…" I reached out for his hands. Defensive, he dug deeper, nails succeeding at carving a slice into his cheek.

Steven screamed.

I caught both hands in mine and held fast. If I didn't, my face could be next. His head thrashed around as he wrestled himself free. Stepping back, I scanned the room for ways to maintain a distance. The couch was a barrier. The bathroom was about twenty steps away. *Get ready.*

Seeing the blood smear on his fingers, Steven's eyes grew big. He found the stinging cut under his eye and called out, "Mommy? Mommy, help me!"

It was broken-picture-geddon again, but shorter. But these events were evolving. Because he and I were together more, I understood him more and feared him less. This time, I *would* wrap him in my arms and settle him onto my lap, cooing and shushing.

"Shhh… Mommy's here. You're going to be okay." I held him tight despite his desperate wiggles to escape. He pinched. He pushed. He bit, spit, and cried louder.

"Sweetie, I want you to feel better. Let's take some breaths." Rocking him and rubbing his back brought the tantrum to a lull. While his tears dried up, my own remained entrenched. I had to be stronger than anything he could serve up.

"He needs to know that his 'very big hurts' don't scare you," Misty advised last week. She was the ultimate voice of reason in my home. "He needs to know there is someone he can bring them to—someone who knows what to do about them."

Well, I didn't always know what to do. But I did my best to be bigger, stronger, quieter, and gentler than the demons in Steven's mind. My steadiness could potentially still his chaos.

The sobs became hiccups and Steven quieted. In that moment, it was just my boy and I, rocking and making eye contact: mother and child. *We made it through!*

"Let's go get a band-aid and try the book again, okay?"

Thankfully, Misty continued making her weekly visits. She would do so until the day we adopted. I don't know what I would have done without her.

The frequency of these snap-rage events didn't drop with our new lifestyle.

"I feel like we're stuck in a loop where he screams and cries and then looks for me to hold him, but *he's* the one who started the fit in the first place, so I'm confused as to why I'm even a part of this." I couldn't keep the shrillness out of my voice. I needed to know how to survive this phase and Misty was my foster fairy godmother. "So, how do I stop this behavior?"

"You don't," she replied. "You keep doing it."

Over and over, I would play a role in Steven's neurological reprogramming. Baby cries: Mommy comes. Baby cries again: Mommy comes again.

Steven was trying to attach!

He was trying to establish an unmistakable pattern between us. Unfortunately, his methods were aggressive and inappropriate for his age.

"But not for his *emotional* age," Misty chimed in. "He's still a baby in many ways, despite the size of his body or the vocabulary he's acquired."

She reminded me that in the grand scheme of things, Steven was making up for many missed developmental milestones that children go through from infancy to maturity. Staying home provided Steven and me an opportunity to dive into the attachment process and explore our relationship. It also opened the door for more promises to be fulfilled.

The first time we met Steven in the dingy Family Services office he once slept in, he asked Ryan and me some very specific questions. After showing him photos of our home and telling him about ourselves, Steven pieced the information together.

"Brian? Can you fix a bike?" He called Ryan by the wrong name all day. We *were* strangers after all.

"Of course. It's my job to know these things." Ryan was enamored already—promising this child the world.

Pressing his lips together and taking a big, nasally breath, Steven asked, "Could you fix mine and teach me how to ride?" Steven received a bicycle from a donation program, but it was broken. The donations were often broken.

When it was my turn for questions, he asked if I could teach him how to read.

"Yes, I can do that."

At seven years old, he could not recognize the twenty-six letters of the alphabet, nor write them. He had no recollection of a mother or father teaching these things, or even reading a book to him. He wanted to know what books said.

Steven weighed the promises as he looked back and forth between us.

"No one's ever helped me with stuff before."

At home, I made every accommodation I could think of to teach Steven the concepts in his lessons. We used everything from pebbles and blocks to shaving cream to keep his sensory demands satiated. It was the most "special" school ever. I let him choose the subjects he wanted to study from a list. I never knew so many things about pirates until then.

This experience opened my eyes to new ways to communicate with my son and approach schoolwork in general. Despite what the traditional school system expected, I learned there are infinite possibilities for showing academic proficiency. Standardized tests and written reports are not the only way for someone to show they have grasped a concept. With my full control over the learning environment, Steven thrived. His intelligence grew exponentially.

Curiously, Steven could perceive numbers *as* numbers, and he grasped mathematical concepts quickly. As a universal language, numbers made sense to him, unlike letters and words, which held too many variations. Steven showed an aptitude for math which resulted in us advancing by seven grade levels in this subject in just over three years.

Mrs. Edwards would have been shocked. We were.

Ryan and I had gone back and forth over medicating Steven to squelch his scattered thoughts and wiggly limbs. I wanted it, he didn't. He wasn't anti-medication, though. His approach was to "wait-and-see," while mine was more like "run-ahead-then-look-back."

"If someone can prove he needs it, *then* I'll consider it."

Otherwise, my complaints about being drained after each school day sounded too similar to "new mom fatigue."

After a particularly long school day learning how to write a complete sentence, Steven was nearly unstoppable. He was spinning, rocking, making sounds, touching things, mumbling words to fill any void in sound. His need to stimulate himself in every imaginable way drove me crazy.

I tried all the suggestions from the Internet to redirect his attention, offer rewards for desired behaviors, and such. We used a sticker chart. More like, it used us.

"Use your words. Let me see your eyes. Good job! Quiet hands."

It was exhausting. He needed pills. Or an exorcism. Or a better teacher. *Maybe, it's me? Maybe, I can't do this.*

The worse his behaviors were, the sadder I felt. The things I tried to keep his attention weren't working. The idea that one day he might actually be able to follow through with a conversation seemed like a dream to me. Maybe, one day, he could complete one page of homework without a meltdown or ten reminders that after question number seven comes question number eight. Maybe he'd remember at least *one* of the four items of clothing he needed to put on in the morning?

Again, I read book after book… after book on how to parent a child with ADHD. Finally, the Little Engine admitted she could not. Love could not cure all.

I made an appointment with a pediatrician.

The day of our appointment, I entered the building crying. Tired and stressed out, I was afraid that if I heard one more "*vrrrrooom… vrrrrooom*" motor sound from my child's mouth, I was going to slap somebody.

"Please… we need help." I might have teetered from fatigue. Steven couldn't make eye contact. He was busy swimming his body through the white paper stretched out over the exam table. It made crunching sounds.

"I believe you," the doctor said. These were words for celebrating. She and I had completed an assessment of behaviors Steven displayed. It was clear to her that a stimulant could help. We got a same-day prescription. Ryan remained skeptical. Of course he would—he didn't read the books.

It took a couple of weeks to get the dosing right, but then one day at the dinner table, our son held a lengthy conversation with us about Star Wars. By this, I mean an exchange of thoughts and ideas which moved forward in logical fashion and built upon each other. There was no baby talk or sound effects. Our meal came to a halt. I looked from Ryan to Steven and back again. *Are you seeing what I'm seeing?*

It was like we were meeting a new person—an expressive boy with thoughts, opinions, ideas, and an incredible recall of movie details. He was funny, too. I didn't know that about him.

The guilt sank in. It tainted the joy and relief that radiated from our eyes and ears. Why did we wait so long to get him medication? This new version of Steven was amazing! And this whole time, he'd just needed a *little* more help.

Chapter 13

Allowing A "Do-Over" In A "Don't Do That" Culture

As foster parents, in addition to restrictions on medical and educational rights, we were not supposed to alter Steven's appearance, diet, or religion. Because of the recent .26 court hearing which severed Steven's biological parents' rights, we could now allow him to explore a new sense of himself. He strongly desired to fit in with our new community and shed the prior reputation he had earned. Life had offered him a fresh start. *Who would Steven become?*

In training, we were indoctrinated into the "Not Yo' Baby" faith. We needed to show the utmost respect for the culture and traditions in which a child was raised. In this "religion," however, you are damned if you do and damned if you don't. The guidelines given could backfire on you from child to child.

We heard stories about how a simple haircut could be enough for the biological family to have the child removed from a foster home. For some cultures, particularly in Native American tribes, hair is symbolic. Don't mess with it.

The primary goal of the foster care system is to reunite families. The "real" happy ending is when biological parents complete their prescribed program of recovery and regain custody of their children again. This being the case, the children would keep their familial culture and identity intact. I completely agree with this principle.

Foster parents need to treat their time with the children like it is a pause button. Only when they are together again with their biological family will their identity formation resume. Of course, this is impractical and nearly impossible in every way. Value systems, moral standards, behavioral norms, and even language is patterned after those we are around—especially in the formative years. Your family and community will no doubt influence the child, just as their prior family did.

Sometimes, this preservation can comfort the child. It can help them feel welcomed and accepted. Perhaps, it can feel like maintaining a thread of connection to their family if they can stick to familiar routines.

Take this with a grain of salt, however. In some cases, bringing up the child's previous way of life can be an emotional trigger. A thoughtful attempt to cook a traditional meal or attend a cultural festival could act as an additional reminder that they are, in fact, separated. Remember the salt? Rub it in.

Foster kids can also meet your innocent show of interest with defensiveness. If you are *not* their family, then who do you think you are intruding on their traditions? Remember, this child you are raising is not *your* baby. They already have a mom and dad and until the .26 hearing is complete, you must assume they will be reunited. Back off.

Recently, I asked Steven what he thought about all the rules we had to follow. He scrunched up his face and tilted his head.

"Just be you and let me be me. Don't cook menudo for me unless you were planning to cook it for yourself anyway. Don't go out of your way because I'm different. That just makes me feel *more* different."

Got it. No menudo.

I think Ryan and I broke every single guideline for what *not* to change prior to the .26 hearing. But to be fair, we were just following Steven's wishes. As long as the changes are child-led and we did not promote or direct them, the biological family could not specifically charge us with contempt (disregard for their parental authority and wishes for the child).

Steven went through a season of soul-searching that threw everyone for a loop. One of the first things he explored was his physical appearance. He cut his hair right away. Right down to the scalp. With craft scissors.

When it grew out again, he cut it again. And dyed it, curled it, spiked it, and clipped bows in it. That's right. The bows and plastic baubles were an important accessory to match his Disney princess dresses. He had superhero and firefighter costumes as well and wore them just as much. Sometimes, he would put on makeup and join me for a manicure or pedicure. He had his own polishes in the Teenage Mutant Ninja Turtle color scheme.

We were looked down on for allowing this.

Mr. Wells famously raised a single eyebrow at us while making his rounds. His visits were not our favorite days of the month. With each, he would remain quizzical as if presented with a new surprise, but never outright asking, "Is this still what you want?"

We also took heat for not doing anything about the cross-dressing problem. That would, however, require us to see it as first: cross-dressing, and second: a problem. I don't see playing dress up as a concerning behavior. Sexuality doesn't even factor into this. If he dressed in animal costumes, few people would conclude he wanted to *become* an animal or get into bestiality. That is ridiculous. We reassured Steven that he could dress however and be whomever in our home.

Out of curiosity, I asked Steven, "Which parents should decide what a kid dresses like?" I expected "biological" or "foster" in reply. He outsmarted me again.

"I don't think that's a fair question. Kids should be able to do what they like with their body." Within reason, son—I agree. I think he meant kids should have freedom to explore and find what makes them happy.

"Yeah. Like, if you want to wear girls' clothes, you can."

Right.

Steven's enthusiastic style was met with disapproval from our community. Not from those who knew us, mind you. Rather, it was people who did *not* know us well who felt the inclination to advise.

One evening, Steven and I were picking up a takeout meal for dinner after a round of appointments. We waited outside the restaurant so Steven could play in the patio area. An older gentleman seated nearby noticed my colorfully dressed son carrying on with his imaginary play. In his glee, Steven extended his arms up and leaned into my torso.

"Mama, carry me!" He was playing "Mommy and Baby," one of our new therapeutic attachment games.

This drew our observer in.

"Can I give you a friendly suggestion?" he implored.

From now on, I'll never say yes to this question.

"Yeah, sure."

"You need to raise that boy properly. Teach him how to be a man and make sure he stops acting like an F-A-G." He spelled it. That way, only *literate people* would be offended, I suppose.

I hadn't expected to hear this in such a woke era. I could have said something like, "Sir, you do *not* know my son." But I didn't. I regret that.

Thankfully, Steven wasn't paying attention.

Some folks took a more direct route to address Steven's appearance.

A woman from our previous church had offered to babysit last-minute. At the end of their time together, she pulled her car up into our driveway to drop him off. Leaning out the car window, she told me about the wonderful things Steven and her son did together. Steven got out and walked around the car towards me but stopped at her voice.

"Show your mom what you learned."

His eyes whipped around to her, then me.

"Go ahead, put your hands on your hips and *say it*." Say what? Did he memorize a Bible verse? What was this about?

"I'm…um," he swallowed. "I'm a boy."

I didn't understand. My supportive "Look what I can do!" smile stuck in place and I hoped there was more to the charade than this.

The woman was unimpressed. Clicking her tongue, she opened the car door and circled her hands at him to go on.

"Try again and say it like you mean it."

My son looked down at the driveway and ground out a more aggressive version.

"That's right!" She cheered and clapped. *What did I just watch?*

Turning, she offered a cheery tidbit of advice, "You need to give him his identity."

The look of shame on my son's face deepened. My suspicions raised. That day she violated my right as a soon-to-be mother by telling Steven how a Godly man should act and look. He did not meet *her* definition.

She got back in the car to leave, calling out once more from the window, "And don't forget to throw away that makeup."

Steven's kept his eyes fixed on the concrete. Quietly, pathetically, he answered to himself, "But I like it."

Following his gaze, I noticed him wiggling his toes in flip-flop sandals. They revealed polish residue from his previously orange and red pedicure. A frown pinned his whole face down.

"Sweetie, what happened?"

"She took my polish off." He sounded wounded.

"Did you give her permission to do this?" He shook his head.

"How do *you* feel about the polish?" I asked, adding, "Does it make you happy?"

"Yeah?" Steven looked up and searched my face, asking if it was okay to like nail polish. That's all I needed to see.

"Then wear it. In this family, we love you no matter what—nail polish or not."

The woman's earlier comment confused me, along with the gentlemen from the restaurant. Is that what other parents think? I have to *tell* Steven who he is to be? If that's the case, I already gave him an identity from day one. My son is loved, accepted, enjoyed, protected, destined, safe and wanted.[25] That is *who he is.*

Besides exploring Steven's outer expression of himself, he also dug a little deeper—skin deep. His cinnamon-spice palette contrasted with Ryan and I's vanilla cream.

"Do I bring up the elephant in the room?" I asked Misty. Steven recently told us he was now White, like us. He even mentioned having red hair, like Mommy's.

"Am I supposed to respond with, 'No, Baby, it's brown hair?'" I asked.

"He knows," she reassured me. "He's expressing a desire to be more like you. He wants people to recognize him as your son. That's validating and feels good."

Since we could not share a skin color, we played with what we could to show an obvious connection—matching outfits. The "Mommy and Me" outfits were a game changer.

Suddenly, we were all wearing the same color scheme. Our family looked like we belonged together… in a Sears photo.

---

25 "Your eyes saw my unformed substance; in your book were written, every one of them, the days that were formed for me, when as yet there was none of them." (Psalms 139:16, English Standard Version)

"I look just like Daddy!" Steven beamed in his khaki shorts and collared polo.

"Yes, you do, Baby. So handsome," I replied.

Steven's new therapist wasn't thrilled with our solution. He was Latino, like Steven.

"We'll need to unpack this behavior a bit *more*," he determined. He had just begun to address Steven's denial of ethnicity. He thought we were dismissing Steven's need for inclusiveness by ignoring his heritage and remaining superficial.

"Look, I know he's grieving over how we are different. There's a clash between his past and his present, and there always *will* be. But I still don't see these behaviors as problematic. They don't need fixing right now."

There is more than one way to make a person feel welcomed into a family and community. Instead of him facing a permanent cultural conflict head-on at the age of seven, what needed to be fixed was our community's response to Steven.

When picking him up from a children's program or class, Ryan and I were being vetted like strangers.

On one occasion, a healthcare provider asked Steven, "Do you know these people?" They said this right in front of Ryan and me. Our family was constantly being reminded that we didn't belong together. These are the kind of encounters Steven wanted to avoid. *These* were the problem behaviors needing fixed.

Ryan and I targeted our community again. By informing healthcare and childcare providers upon our first meeting we were a multicultural family built through adoption, they responded more positively. We made ourselves more visible in our community as *that* family. We made our needs for help, accommodations, and privacy clear to those who were new to us.

Sometimes these disclosures were in front of Steven, but we made a point to have most done in private, in advance, if possible. For example, before we went to one of Ryan's social functions at work, we prepped several coworkers on some of the anxieties Steven had. By educating more people around us to use the word "son," instead of "foster son," Steven became noticeably more comfortable and confident. He hesitated less when calling out to "Mom" or "Dad" in social settings because fewer people questioned the connection between us. By being outspoken about our family structure, Ryan and I created a more comfortable and accepting world for our son.

Even though, for a few years, it was second nature to explain our family to people we met, I forgot ever-so-often, like when we hired an algebra tutor for Steven's accelerated work.

After the third tutoring session, the gentleman stopped in our doorway to ask in hushed tones, "Does he know?"

"Know what? That he's gifted?" Earlier, he asked what school Steven had been attending because he'd never worked with a 10-year-old on high school math before. I giggled at his shock.

"No. That he's adopted."

This time, it was I who raised my eyebrows.

Chapter 14

What Is "Normal?"

"*Does he know?*"

This time, the speaker was a thin, friendly looking man who had just come from the bus stop at our neighborhood park. Steven was happily playing with a friend we were babysitting. They were the only two kids in the area at that time.

"Does he know what?" I pondered. The last time I checked, I had no idea how to answer this question.

The stranger clarified.

"Does he know he has something? That… that he isn't normal?"

The question momentarily stumped me. "Normal" is subjective, but asking a mother if her child is normal is definitely rude.

"Oh, you mean his autism? Yes, he knows." Thankfully, it was enough to end the conversation. It's rather unsatisfactory to gossip over common knowledge.

Righteous anger aside, there was no point in denying Steven's autism. A stranger could see it from a hundred feet away. Also, there has never been any shame or secrecy attached to his diagnosis in our family. Steven was well aware.

Over the years, I'd heard several opinions on why it's best to keep children unaware of their differences. Disabilities are only hidden abilities. Everyone is special and you can do anything. No one loses. *Trophies for all!*

I'd been directed to stories of Isaac Newton, Albert Einstein, and Thomas Edison. Supposedly, they were on the autism spectrum as well. They were never medically or therapeutically treated, but "Look how great they turned out!" Sure, but what about their personal lives? They weren't known for being kind and loving people with successful relationships. I wanted those things for my son.

It begs the question: *What if they knew?* What if they had received medical and community supports to assist them with social skills, time management, and other executive functions? If the diagnosis existed back then, and they had caring and dedicated therapists, parents, and teachers who taught them a better way to relate and express themselves, just imagine the astronomical impact this might have had on their lives.

Both Ryan and I felt it was important to communicate to Steven that the diagnoses stacked against him would never change the way we felt about him. However, they needed to be managed, and he needed to become self-aware so he can cope with the added challenges of life. For example, he would need to take his therapies and medications seriously.

Some things which are easy for other kids are extraordinarily difficult for him, and he needs to know how to find help or use workarounds in those situations. In contrast, his giftedness could be used as a competitive advantage and should be highlighted. And we have always taught him that none of his disabilities or diagnoses could never be used as an excuse to not be the best version of himself.

As parents, we felt responsible for equipping Steven to do his best and eventually become his own advocate. Isn't that what all loving mothers and fathers want for their children? *The best?*

"Misty," I implored. "What do I do with all of these confused and angry thoughts? What do I say to people with stupid comments? How do I keep *my* life from being swallowed up by *Steven's*?" Because of our forthright communication style, we were unintentionally inviting people in our community to ask more questions than we were ready to answer.

By being more transparent, we weren't *just* the Molonys anymore. We were doing something difficult and conspicuous. People watched to see what would happen next.

Misty would end her weekly visits once the adoption was finalized. They were a crutch I would soon lose. Each conversation offered me encouragement, a sense of normalcy, and an opportunity to bring up some of the most awful things we had experienced that week without judgment. She was my safe person.

I didn't want to be abandoned to my thoughts when she left. I honestly thought there wasn't a single person in the world that could relate to me when it came to parenting a child like Steven. Of course, I was wrong.

"Two things," she started. "You're not alone. There are support groups for foster and adoptive parents. Join one. You'd be surprised how common and relatable your experiences are." She was right.

"And, as far as your thoughts go… start writing them down. Designate a place to get them out each day and don't look back." She made a very good point about not using my husband as a dumping ground for my frustrations. It was a destructive habit that sounded like whining or regret.

There was no regret in my heart. Never has been. But there *were* some days where I wrote whatever came to my mind freely as if they were personal letters to Pandora, the mythological keeper of monsters and dark secrets.

Looking back at the journal entries, against Misty's advice, proved how isolation during tough times can drive a person virtually insane.

Ryan and I's first visit to a foster-adoptive family support group still holds a fond place in my heart. We weren't sure how much of the "craziness" we were dealing with was kosher to say aloud. Then the *other* parents spoke.

When they began their "How was your week?" speech, my jaw dropped. These people were in deep! My perspective quickly changed and I went from feeling misunderstood to laughing over IEP meetings, soiled carpets, and social worker drama as if it was all completely normal. For us, it was.

In this group, we shared our battle scars and celebrated accomplishments that other families might achieve in one week with their biological child, but for one of us, it took eight months.

"Could you believe what that other couple went through?" Ryan asked. "It's crazy to even think about." I agreed with a slow nod.

Each session offered Ryan and me a chance to gauge how we were holding up, but with realistic, peer-defined expectations. The leveled playing field gave us hope for a win.

I thought, if *those* people can get through *that*, then I'm going be alright.

As would our son.

The support groups we attended sometimes felt like parenting classes. Other times, we just vented over cheap pizza. Many felt similar to a grief support group or an addiction recovery program. There was no official diagram, but we were all working our way through the Seven Stages of Foster-Adoptive Parenting:[26]

1. **Ambition / False Hope:** I think I can do this! How difficult can it be? I took the classes and passed my background check. I'm ready—bring on the kids.
2. **Denial / Disassociation:** These problems? Oh, they probably won't last. We can ride this out. We're just getting settled in. The kid will learn our system eventually. Let's see how next week goes.
3. **Doubt / Fear:** Hmm, this situation wasn't mentioned in training. I'm not sure how to approach this. Am I doing this right? The kid doesn't seem to be responding like I hoped. What did I get myself into?
4. **Anger / Bargaining:** Now I realize this isn't working. The situation hasn't improved. I didn't know how bad it could

---

26 This is a modified version of the Kübler-Ross model of the five stages of grief. I make no claims to having expertise in the field of psychiatry. This list is strictly for entertainment value. Actual model is from the book reference below.

Kübler-Ross, E. *On Death And Dying*. New York, NY: Collier Books get. I didn't agree to this kind of thing. Somebody needs to do something about this!

5. **Burnout / Depression:** No matter what I do, the kid is who they are, and I am who I am. I clearly cannot do this well. Nothing is working. I'm hurting, tired, and scared. The kid deserves better.
6. **Self-Care / Hope:** I need help.[27] I *have* to find a way to manage my stress. I need to find someone to talk to—someone who understands me. Being more open feels good. The kid is responding to me in a different way.
7. **Advocacy / Acceptance:** I realize what my priorities are. My emotional stability is being noticed by others. It's encouraging to others.[28] The kid is now working with me and we have seen progress. I believe we can do this together.

As a group, we were learning to not place the burden of finding joy and self-worth on the children we cared for. A total family transformation was supposed to be parent-initiated. The secret ingredient for a long-lasting emotional connection to a child who has been in foster care was to deal with your *own* personal baggage.

As foster parents, we need to be mindful of our contribution to the relationship; observing our own emotional triggers, attachment

---

27 "Not only that, but we also rejoice in our sufferings, because we know that suffering produces perseverance; perseverance, character; and character, hope. And hope does not disappoint us, because God has poured out His love into our hearts through the Holy Spirit, whom He has given us." (Romans 5: 3-5, Berean Study Bible)

28 "Each time he said, 'No. But I am with you; that is all you need. My power shows up best in weak people.' Now I am glad to boast about how weak I am; I am glad to be a living demonstration of Christ's power, instead of showing off my own power and abilities." (2nd Corinthians 12:9, The Living Bible)

styles, and general bias and expectations. By doing so, we can be less defensive, more proactive, and more compassionate parents. I would say more on this topic, but there are already more than 4,000 books written by experts. Go find one.[29]

29 Topics you may wish to search under include Trust-Based Parenting, Whole-Brain Child, Attachment Parenting, and Trauma-Informed Parenting.

Chapter 15

A Child By Any Other Name...

Of all the lifestyle changes we have explored with Steven, the following was the hardest to work with—especially since it began immediately after Steven had been officially placed with us long-term, but still, long before we confirmed out decision to adopt. We mentioned that he could stay forever, if he wanted to. And we were open to adopting him, if that was something he agreed to.

He immediately agreed.

Ryan and I tried to be the very best versions of *ourselves* while Steven began a process of renaming himself. This is highly frowned-upon behavior from a foster youth. It reflects emotional instability similar to a mid-life crisis.

Steven and I had been reading about Moses from the Old Testament in the Bible.[30] This character was adopted. As we read through the end of the story, another character was introduced. This man, Joshua, did not show reluctance or fear when he was asked to go conquer and live in a new land. He had no reason to fear this big change in his life because God set into a motion a series of events that would secure Joshua's win. That got Steven thinking.

"Mommy? Can I change my name to Joshua when I'm adopted?" This came as a surprise to me.

"Um, sure, if that's what you want. But why?"

He thought for a moment, then came up with, "It's a good name."

"So, you want it to be like Joshua in the Bible?"

"Maybe." His eyes lit up curiously. "I want God to go into battle with me."

Ryan and I hadn't put too much thought into changing his name prior to this. Perhaps a name change would be easy if we were adopting an infant or toddler, but Steven was old enough to speak for himself on the matter. However, we weren't sure he was *mature* enough to understand the weight of the decision.

I can understand the practice of adoptive parents renaming an infant. Their desire to gift the child with a familial or symbolic name is relatable. But an older child changing his own name was a deeper, more complex expression not necessarily of joining into a family, but of separating from one. This was much more serious than idolizing a Bible character.

As a mother, my heart would ache forever if I knew my child knowingly replaced the name I gave them at birth.

---

30 Moses' story begins in Exodus, Chapter 2. Joshua's story begins in Exodus, Chapter 33.

Ryan and I decided to ask for more authoritative counsel on this issue. Mr. Wells was careful with his words.

"This isn't a good thing." His response was reminiscent of the time Steven asked to call us "Mom" and "Dad."

"He's going through many changes right now, which he might *say* he understands and wants, but he doesn't. Not really." Mr. Wells explained how Steven might be feeling lost and confused. He might have been bringing these changes to our attention as a way to signal for help.

Ryan and I were supposed to keep him grounded—to slow him down and reassure him that not everything about him had to change because of an adoption. In his way, Steven was asking us, "Who am I now? How am I supposed to behave as your son? What am I supposed to do about the other family I still have?"

He was looking for instructions on how to be adopted.

In his mind, he had to leave everything behind: his parents, his siblings, his culture, and now, his name. By making himself into someone new—someone he thought we liked or approved of—he was creating the outward image of a new family before the internal attachments were fully realized. After all, Steven hadn't quite yet said "I love you" to *either* of us at this point.

Steven wanted a family so badly he was rushing the process.

Maybe.

Steven's therapist also had strong words on the matter. By the time he confronted us about Steven's request, though, Steven was already dead-set on a new name.

Ryan and I had not discouraged Steven's search. He explored his options for several weeks, here and there, beginning with simple variations on his original name. For example, "Steven" became "Steve," which then switched to "Shawn" the following week. "Shawn" stuck for a while, then evolved into "Shane," "Dane," and "Dave." Every once in a while, he'd revisit a name in the rotation to really confuse us.

With the playful back-and-forth, we were not sure how serious he was about this. We set some ground rules, however, to limit the confusion in our household. Each day, Steven needed to tell us which name he wanted to be called and we'd all agree to use it. Most importantly, Steven needed to respond to it. Otherwise, he ended up ignoring us while we ran through a list of names, calling out to him as if we had eleven children already.

One day, we were out at the pool with friends. Steve-Dane-Dave was breaking pool etiquette by splashing too much and trying to carry his friends around. Typical boy nonsense, if you will.

The teen lifeguard called out from his tower, "No splashing." Nothing registered with my child. It could have been a general statement to the masses, to be fair. The teen waved his arms and tried again with the red megaphone.

"*Blue Suit!* Put your friend down." That one was clear. I knew exactly who "Blue Suit" was. Leaving my mom friend and our sticky, plastic recliners, I walked to the ledge of the pool and called out as well.

"Dave. Daaaave!" Nothing—not even a head tilt acknowledged my call.

"Steven, stop it!" I tried again.

"Hey, Dane! It's time to get out." No response. Frustrated, I mumbled a curse. I was fairly certain I had used the name-of-the-day, but checked my mental Rolodex anyway. Looking back at my friend, she was watching this performance with a cross of amusement and annoyance. I knew the moment I returned, she would remind me of how stupid this name game was. Even the lifeguard was giving me looks now.

I clenched my teeth and narrowed my gaze on *whatever-his-name-was.*

It was time to get in the pool.

"Steven is trying to recreate himself," the therapist explained. The day's session was over and Steven was absent-mindedly playing with the lobby toys.

"Yeah, we know," I answered. I didn't like his pretentious tone. Be aware: therapists are supposed to help, not judge. But they have a bias, emotional baggage, and triggers just like any other person. I thought I was using this to our advantage.

I thought finding a male therapist with Steven's cultural background could help Steven feel more comfortable opening up and exploring his trauma and loss. In retrospect, this was an ineffective approach to hiring. The best therapist he has ever worked with looked nothing like him. She focused on supporting the whole family as a unit, rather than individuals being cobbled together through adoption.

"This could be a sign of hyper-vigilance. He is constantly trying to please the new parents out of necessity. It's a survival strategy," he continued.

"But we don't ask him to do those things," I replied. "We haven't initiated the changes or interfered with his choices." His conclusion needed some "unpacking," in my opinion. If a child is free to be whomever they dream to be and is provided a fertile environment to grow and explore, "survival," as he mentioned, absolutely *will* happen, but not in the way he implied. Not only that, but my son was thriving.

"I see. But, by supporting the changes he makes, you are essentially rewarding him for the behavior."

There was logic in his conclusion. But then he went on. He strongly advised us to stop encouraging Steven's exploration. By continuing, he believed we were inadvertently dishonoring his past life, disregarding it, even. We were "taking something away" from him via good intentions.

"What if, when he is an adult, he regrets the name change and grieves the loss?" He asked me this in all seriousness, but never waited for an answer.

"He'll look at you as the person who made the change. *You're* the adult in the situation. You have the ability to stop this."

I didn't appreciate the guilt-bomb. That night Ryan *was* the recipient of my frustrations. Were we making a mistake?

Ryan laughed out loud.

"What do *I* have to do with the name he picks? When he's an adult, he can change it back if he wants. Or pick something new. I don't care. I'll love him no matter what he is called."

My champion: unconflicted. Ryan never wavered when it came to this boy.

"What about… all the other stuff?" I doubted. Ryan cupped his hands on my cheeks, gently caressing my jawbone. With soft eyes on mine, Ryan directed his words to my heart.

"Sweetie, listen. Gay, straight, blue jeans or dresses… what I see is my son, just as he is. I love him. And I love you. That's what matters."

Eventually, Steven settled on a name. He asked us to help him make it official. Around friends and family it wasn't a problem to continue playing along. But this was hard to do in clinical situations.

"Sweetie, you *have* to understand that when we go to the doctor, you will still need to respond to 'Steven,'" I explained. He cringed at the last appointment when the *wrong* name was announced in the waiting room.

"There's not much more I can do right now. Until you're adopted, your name is still legally 'Steven.'" Steven was unsatisfied with my explanation. He pouted over this for a few days. It felt horrible to remind him the adoption wasn't official, yet. But in *his* mind, it was.

"Mommy?" He came up to my bedroom while I happened to be journaling in bed. My mind was a little cloudy.

"Yes, Baby?" I sighed. I looked once more at the document I was typing, then saved the file and set the laptop computer aside. He stood in the doorway watching me. He knew I was writing my thoughts. I had told him how it made me feel better.

Taking a step forward, he asked, "Can I write something?" Huh. Something was off.

"I suppose so," I replied. "What's on your mind?"

I waved a mental hand to clear the clouds above my head and make room for the ones he was dragging over.

"I want to write a letter," he began.

"Okay. To who?"

"My mom."

That didn't feel good. I didn't like where this was going. His biological mother was unreachable for good, but a part of her would always be with him. It made me jealous.

"Baby, you know we can't..."

"I know, I know," he waved *his* hands to "slow my horses."

His tone deepened. "It's not a *real* letter, Mommy. I just need to write it. Please."

At seven years old, he couldn't type, so I was automatically his scribe.

Dear Mom,
I love you.

I had *such* a love-hate relationship to this letter. I admired his tender emotion and openness towards his biological mother. I wished that one day I would be the recipient of it as well. But this moment isn't about me, so I'll step back.

Mom, I'm sad about all the bad stuff that happened. You know...

I hope you are safe now. I miss you.

I'm seven now. I'm getting tall and I'm doing alright in school. I'm good at math.

He looked at me, then resumed.

I have a wonderful new mom and dad. They are very nice to me.

You weren't. You were kind of a...

"Mom, can I use the B-word?" He asked. Yikes! Way to put me on the spot, kid. I did my best to stay neutral.

"It's not my letter. Say what you need to say."

I think you would like my new parents.

By the way, I'm changing my name. It's David now. D-A-V-I-D.

I don't need my old one anymore.

Chapter 16

And Then It Got Worse

David's recent writing activity seemed to have released him from a terrible burden. He freed himself to share an innermost desire in a *very* official, validating way. But it didn't stop there. With an emotional win under his belt, David began sharing more of his past with us. He recalled memories—both good and bad. He regaled us with tales of his siblings and the oddball situations they got themselves into. I helped him write many of them down to preserve those precious memories in his own journal. David would miss his siblings forever.

Writing and storytelling were wonderful bonding activities that brought us closer together. They showed progress in our relationship. Some might call it therapeutic or even healing. Making sense out of our past helps us to move beyond it; relieving stress and eliminating the need to ruminate.[31] But as David's storytelling confidence increased, his tales took on a heavier tone.

Before we continue down this darkened path, there is some housekeeping to attend to. I've reduced the content of this chapter to maintain a certain boundary between telling *my* story and telling *his*. I share only a limited understanding of events, which is clouded with emotion. What I have written is currently the best I can do to express how I felt upon hearing his tales.

While my son's journal was filled with expositions, my own was saturated with tears of depression, hopelessness, fear, crushing pain and heartache that I cannot include here.[32] I am still angered and sickened, years later, from what I've learned of his past and have cried, ached, and spent sleepless nights over this chapter.

My actual journal entries are filled with fractured thoughts, inappropriate language, and Bible verses that read like a wrinkled

---

31 A 2012 study by surgeons regarding writing therapy as a beneficial medical intervention compiled several physical changes in patients who are treated via traditional practices with and without therapeutic writing as a co-treatment. Recorded effects of the patients who completed writing therapy exercises included improved cognition, lower blood pressure, lessened pain levels, reduced anxiety and depressive symptoms, improved respiratory and digestive functions, and fewer behavioral problems in children with Post-Traumatic Stress Disorder.

Mugerwa, S., Holden, J. (2012, Dec.). Writing therapy: a new tool for general practice? *British Journal of General Practice. 62(*605), 661-663.

32 "The righteous cry out, and the Lord hears them; he delivers them from all their troubles. The Lord is close to the brokenhearted and saves those who are crushed in the spirit. A righteous man may have many troubles, but the Lord delivers him from them all; He protects all his bones, not one of them will be broken." (Psalm 34: 17-20 New International Version)

religious tract from the street gutter that screams of salvation and damnation. That being the case, I chose to communicate through poetry, composed in partnership with and by the express approval of my son.

Ryan and I had a lot of ideas about what went on in David's life "before us," but we had not dug deep enough within ourselves to consider the extent of the trauma endured. David spoke of starvation, beatings, verbal abuse, and witnessing drug and alcohol use as if it was any ol' day—compounded and reinforced as "the way things were." In less than his seven years, he experienced every type of life-shortening trauma that the Adverse Childhood Experience (ACE) survey can calculate.[33] Theoretically, the likelihood of him committing suicide because of the experiences is one thousand percent higher than a child without those experiences.

Tragically, none of the stories David shared with Ryan or I would stand out as any more remarkable than what we'd heard from other foster families in our support group. When hearing about other families' experiences, however, there was a certain emotional safety involved. We were shocked, sickened maybe, but not destroyed. Relief follows.

33 The ACE score evaluates ten types of personal and social traumas that, if experienced in childhood, will negatively and measurably impact one's physical and mental health. Manifestations of the stress include heart and lung disease, cancer, autoimmune disorders, domestic violence, substance abuse, depression and suicidal thinking. More information can be found on the Center for Disease Prevention's webpage (https://www.cdc.gov/violenceprevention/childabuseandneglect/acestudy).

"Thank God I'm not in *that* situation." Then, as a listener, you move on.

The hard stuff isn't so hard when you're in the cheap seats, distanced from the action. When you're the one in the arena, however, the pain and damage are intense. The consequences of a child's past could forcibly change a foster parent's life for worse. Ryan and I were not adequately prepared to experience what is referred to as secondary, or vicarious trauma. It is destructive, visceral, and has required ongoing professional help for both of us.

When someone or something has hurt your baby… there's no telling what thoughts you may have to wrestle. As painful as the effects may be, however, we must recognize that they are *nothing* like the child's experience.

You'll lose sleep, as your child did, but less than they did. You'll feel betrayed and enraged, but not as much as they were. And your mind will wander in sadness, echoing "Why?" and "How could this happen?"

In the past, when things got messy, David couldn't help or defend himself. He may have had nowhere to turn and no one to help him heal. But we were here for him now. As mature and informed adults, foster parents should be able to find helpful resources and compartmentalize stress. We are *supposed* to be equipped to handle this stuff. According to our "parent" job description, it was our responsibility to get into the child's mess, organize the mess, and in time, help walk them out of the mess. It's a dirty job not many sign up for.

Inside.
I have to write so I don't go crazy.
I know it will help, but my thoughts are hazy.
There's a ringing and a pain; a lot of pressure on my brain.
My eyes dart through the air as if I'll find answers there.
No tears have fallen as of yet. They'll be here soon, I would bet.
I'm honored that you've chosen me to share in your great secrecy.
A darkened truth... neglect... abuse... Now, what do I do with this story?

"No! Please don't close the door!" David needed to use the bathroom then take a shower. I didn't understand the big deal about closing the door. He was always leaving doors open around the house and never gave me a moment to myself unless I was in the bathroom. And sometimes, not even then. I needed one less battle for the day. Bedtime was coming soon and his PTSD would wage war again.

Shrugging my shoulders, I swung it open and told him this time it was fine, Mommy would be elsewhere, should he need me. We knew that he should be comfortable bathing himself without assistance by now. It was a hurdle we *thought* we overcame. His face drooped into a sorrowful puddle, bottom lip quivering.

"Momma, don't leave me, please."

"What are you talking about? I'll be downstairs."

"No, no, no... Please don't go!" The quivers upgraded to strangled sobs and stinging tears ready to overflow at any moment. I knew if I took one step backward, he'd fall apart again. Was this separation anxiety? We homeschooled. We were not "separated" for several days.

Ryan and I placated the door demands for weeks, sitting next to the bathtub and reading children's books or chatting with David about his day. Sometimes it was necessary to be near and make sure he washed the essentials. He was still afraid to immerse his head in the water.

We took turns being held captive in the small space. Eventually, I scooted farther from the tub's edge to mid-bathroom. Perhaps, I sat against the wall with a book, hoping my imagination could help me escape. Maybe I wiped the mirrors and sink—anything to be in proximity, but far less entertaining. Sometimes we were trapped in there for an hour, mentally cataloging all the other things we could be doing.

Time after time, we inched closer to the door. It seemed to be the gateway to fresh air and fun. I could hear Ryan watching TV downstairs without me. Conversely, Ryan heard me return home from walking the dog, laughing over a phone call with a friend.

We had a private celebration between us when we could sit in the doorway without David's anxiety skyrocketing. Finally, we made it just outside the door—still within earshot, never truly free.

"Are you still there?" David called out with urgency.

"Yes," Ryan replied. "I was here two minutes ago. I'm still here now."

He was on duty while I passed by to start the laundry. Ryan slouched down with his knees bent, elbows propped atop and head hanging. The perfect picture of a prisoner without shackles.

"How long is this going to take?" He looked up, indicating the door with his head. "We've been doing this way too long. He's not a baby. He can shower himself."

We both knew that to be true. But the daily torment was never about the shower.

What must it have been
When you were alone, locked in?
Did you feel singled-out and jealous?
Were you in the light or was it darkness?
The space must have closed tightly on your chest.
In panic, I wonder if you could ever find rest?
Or, did you imagine escaping and eating?
Or, did you imagine avoiding a beating?
Was it safer to be inside?
Was it better to die?
This is no way to live.
I'd go out of my mind,
Just as you did.

I thought to myself, if I experienced just *one* facet of this child's story, how long would it take me to recover my trust in humanity? A few months? Two years? Never? How long would doubt sit in my bones? But upon hearing his story, a pile of paperwork was now due. I had no time to think more on this.

As mandated reporter, we were required to disclose all knowledge of child abuse. The reason why David was afraid of closed doors was shared with the authorities and added to his file with the state. In an e-mail from Mr. Wells regarding the notification, we were told the following:

> *"It's a big deal, but not as big as it seems. It's very common to hear tragic stories revealed as children become more comfortable in a placement and begin to attach. This is what progress looks like. Be prepared: the safer he feels, the more he'll say."*

It didn't take long for David to feel safer. As long as we listened, he continued to talk.

From Small Eyes.

The house
was very big.
People came and they went
carrying in gift boxes and out lunch sacks.
Some would stay around all day, always looking out,
carrying guns and counting the stacks.
The door was knocked.
They tried to run.
She helped the cops.
He punched and swung.
We thought they were friends but someone there was baited.
Under the table, there I hid. Near tape and baggies, I waited.

"Misty, it just keeps coming out," I vented.

For today's visit, we sat near the sliding glass door to watch David draw with sidewalk chalk on the back patio. I didn't want him to overhear the conversation. I read the child's-eye account to her and asked for help making sense of it.

"What does this even mean? It sounds like he's describing a drug bust! The details are a little off and I'm grasping to fill in the blanks," I whined. Ryan and I had tried to be understanding and patient listeners, not overreacting with our facial expressions or too many glances to each other while David shared his memories over dinner. At these meal times, it was Ryan and I who were the lite eaters.

We followed the advice of the social workers to not press David for further information. But after dinner felt like a crime scene investigation. We exchanged notes, searched the Internet for any names mentioned, and tried to piece together a cohesive picture from the day's revelations.

David was drawing the outline of a chalk road for his toy cars to race on. Blue-tinged dust was on his little palm and on one side of his face when he came up to wave "Hello" through the glass. He was happy today. Misty watched me as I watched him, smiling back and nodding my own greeting. He returned to his project, revealing two orange ovals of dust on the seat of his checkered shorts. *He couldn't be cuter.*

Looking over to Misty, a compassionate smile rested on her face.

"Janelle, just stay curious and available to listen anytime he's ready to talk. Try to validate his truth and experience *however* he remembers it. Remember, you're hearing stories from a little boy with a limited vocabulary. As he gets older, some memories may fade. Some might get clearer. Who knows at this point?"

Misty cautioned me to be mindful of my own interpretations and emotional reactions. It would not make much sense for David if I reacted more strongly to his experiences than he did. I wasn't there and it didn't happen to me.

"So… Let it soak in, rather than wring it out?" I offered wryly. Besides writing, humor was my coping skill at the time.

She saw right through it.

"Janelle, it's okay to wonder if this is too much. It's more common than you think, especially as the reality of his abuse begins to unfold."

Begins? *How could there be more?* She wasn't a mind reader, but she might as well have been. Her sage advice continued.

"Now's a good time to have an honest and possibly difficult conversation with Ryan. The weight of the commitment has increased, and doubts will arise."

If only Ryan were there so I *didn't* have to have this conversation again.

"What do we do, then… if there is more?" My voice was more hollow than I would like to admit.

Misty heard both of the questions I asked: how to move forward and how to quit. She answered both.

"It will take a lifetime of new, positive experiences to outweigh the old. The goal for you two, now, is to come to a place of acceptance with your decision."

Forever loving this child as-is, knowing *even more* was bound to be revealed, was a steep request. Not from Misty, mind you, but from deep within ourselves.

One year prior, we were confidently rejecting children's profiles that listed the disabilities David has and the situation he was in. We were guarding our hearts and home *against* children who were considered tough cases. But now we faced almost every demon of doubt in one small package.

Acceptance, in this case, would mean consciously acknowledging that this child has a life that began before us, and there is nothing in our power we can do to change a single detail.

But that was over now. A new story had begun, and in this one, we could do *everything* in our power to set our child on a different trajectory. We could put him on a path of hope and healing.

Acceptance did not, however, require us to approve of what was done to him. It is not an offer of forgiveness, either, though this is a good goal to set in terms of spiritual growth. I still wrestle with this as more comes out in therapy, years later.

Knowing that I could deal with my anger and grief slowly helped me to feel more comfortable with moving forward.

Acceptance also meant not giving in to the fear of becoming a statistic. I still believed in God's plan and promise for our family. We were not giving up on a child who deserved to be loved and cared for. For better or worse, we loved David.

Nothing he told us could change that now.

Unspeakable.

He told me it didn't hurt.
It didn't hurt?
But Baby, it does. It was pervert!
It's shattering my mind and I'm about to use a shard
or two to hurt them back in kind.

It didn't hurt.
What kind of person does that...
To a little boy... My baby boy.

He would do as you told for years, not saying a word,
then the words would pour out
like hot oil in my ears.

What didn't hurt?
I wish I could say it.
To name it, shame it, and even fillet it.
But the act and impact still make me feel sick. It doesn't deserve the space on my lips.

My heart sank to a new low.

Chapter 17

Every Wound: Opened

God, grant me the serenity to accept the things I cannot change, courage to change the things I can, and wisdom to know the difference.[34]

After hearing all that, I had never felt so helpless in my life. Admittedly, I spent a good chunk of time thinking that my child was ruined or damaged goods, somehow. The losses from his past were translating to loss in his future.

This line of thinking contradicted what I knew to be true of people in general. Pasts can shape futures, or leave an imprint, but the future is still new and fresh. Worrying about yesterday and tomorrow would never bring me any closer to a solution. Both are out of my reach.

---

34 The Serenity Prayer, originally written by Reinhold Niebuhr (1892–1971).

In my daily quiet time, I returned to my faith to provide direction. Again, God and Ryan were the only outlets I had. At this time, David's history was on legal lockdown, considered confidential to the state and contained within his circle of social workers and medical professionals. Not my son: not my right to speak.

Keeping these secrets inside myself was like forming a physical bond with the immortal Pandora herself. I now held a box of my own. In it was boiling magma and searing steam that would eventually cool and harden into an iceberg. I had never felt so "shut up" before. I stopped singing at church. I stopped participating in social groups. I just knew if I tried to make a new friend, the craziness would leak out and scare everyone away.

After the adoption, I remember trying out a book club for women at the new church we were attending. I didn't know any of the ladies there because I turned myself into a mute. But now that the adoption was finalized, I *could* talk. I could share my story, his story ...our story.

"Hi, my name is Janelle." (*GULP.*) I didn't wait for a reply. "I, um, I'm a new mom. My kid has some major mental problems. I don't know how to deal with this. I'm sad a lot. I have no friends," I paused to look up from my hands and take a breath. "I'm really glad to be here."

I made no friends that day, but the ice was beginning to melt.

I wish I could tell you that I had an unshakable faith, but as you've witnessed, it wasn't like that.[35] In order to steady myself, I

35 "'Though the mountains be shaken and the hills be removed, yet my unfailing love for you will not be shaken, nor my covenant of peace be removed from you,' says the Lord, who has compassion on you." (Isaiah 54:10, New International Version)

had to *continuously* seek answers through God.[36] It was necessary to keep my eyes and my mind fixed on His absolute knowledge and sovereignty.[37] I depended on daily reminders that He was still a good God with good plans.[38]

In this process of clinging to my Savior, the energy in our home began to shift. David started asking me to find Bible verses for *him* to memorize. He started repeating the words he'd overheard in my prayers. David was claiming healing and forgiveness for his own life when he prayed. And before we knew it, Ryan was being invited to pray *with* David before bed.

This was no small detail to be overlooked. Though Ryan and I had been together for almost a decade, he had a minimal understanding of the Christian faith. He'd been to church with me only a handful of times. He showed polite respect for my beliefs and nothing more. It was the way it was.

But the tide was shifting.[39]

---

36 "Seek first the kingdom of God and all these things will be given unto you." (Matthew 6:33, New International Version)

37 "But my eyes are fixed on You, oh God, my Lord; in You I seek refuge; do not leave my soul defenseless." (Psalm 141:8, Berean Study Bible)

38 "Trust in the Lord with all your heart and lean not on your own understanding; in all your ways submit to Him and He will make your paths straight." (Proverbs 3:5-6, New International Version)

39 "He reached down from on high and took hold of me; he drew me out of deep waters." (2nd Samuel 22:17, New Living Translation)

"Mom?" He had that watchful look on his face. It was time for another important chat. "There's going to be a baptism at the church next week."

"Oh, yeah?" I wasn't sure if he knew what that meant. The topic piqued my curiosity. "What about it?"

David and I had been going to church alone for several months. Ryan was *always* too busy or too tired to attend. He frequently accepted work on the weekends as another way to avoid the matter. Without proper childcare at home, David had to come along.

David had mentioned that a previous foster family had taken him to church sometimes, so he wasn't against it. For me to direct David towards any religion was yet another foster rule breaker. Again, this was a matter of "childcare."

"I want to do it," he announced.

"Be baptized?" I smirked. I wondered if his true intent was to go swimming. The ceremony would be held at the same place that had a toddler splash pad he enjoyed. Only a mega church would rent out an *entire* waterpark to perform a few hundred baptisms in an afternoon. It would be an epic pool party, for sure.

David was much more serious than I assumed.

"Yeah. The Bible says that we can get born again and have a fresh life. [40] I want that." He spoke with joy and anticipation. On that note, I signed him up.

The message of forgiveness, rebirth, and a forever loving father resonated with David. Even with the sensory overload in his kids' class… even when he was sucking his thumb while I rocked him

40 "This means that anyone who belongs to Christ has become a new person. The old life is gone; a new life has begun!" (2nd Corinthians 5:17, New Living Translation)

in the back of the main auditorium… he was listening. Yes, we eventually migrated to a seat where we could pace back and forth along the far wall of the church, sit on the floor in a private picnic, or I could hold him in my arms and gently bounce. Now the only person we would annoy was the pastor on stage.

In support of David's request, Ryan agreed to come with us to watch the baptism. I also enlisted him to be the parent who would be responsible for getting in the water with David, should he need assistance. I was the better photographer between us so logically, I had to stay dry.

David still wouldn't put his head underwater for more than a split second to rinse a little shampoo out. We knew there'd be an awakening of a different sort when they dunked him. *Thanks, Ryan.*

The day of the ceremony, Ryan patiently sat through the sermon and volunteered to hold David when he squirmed. After the conclusion of the message, we were directed to head over to the waterpark. David remained excited and determined to see this through. Until we arrived.

Imagine ten booming speakers on stands, theatrical lights on towers, cheering and pushing crowds, and colorful balloons bobbing from every ramada. Folks dressed in all black carried large cameras and even larger video cameras to follow the crowd around and document the day. The weather was perfect. Cloudy and warm.

Stadium stands were erected on three sides of the main pool. David's goody bag included instructions for which side of the pool to enter. Today, groups of participants were going to be baptized in unison by pastoral teams.

David freaked out (to put it lightly).

This event was far removed from my own childhood baptism in a church of two hundred people. I climbed into a shallow bathtub hidden behind a false wall on the stage, dipped down, fully dressed, into the lukewarm water, then went back to my childrens' class after a brisk toweling off. No swimsuit for me. That would have been too sexy.

Sweat beaded on Ryan's forehead as he wrangled a fussy child trying to pull his arm out of his grasp. David looked like he was ready to bolt. It was as if the pool deck beneath him was electrified and he had to keep jumping to save his life.

No, no, no… *No freakin' way*. Ryan was giving me the "Let's get out of here" look. But we came here for a reason! This was David's moment.

We couldn't let the sensory processing disorder and fear of water defeat his dream. I did some quick thinking, but not much. My plan was impulsive at best and I was sure I'd be heading for trouble.

I knew approaching the pastor was breaking protocol. He usually had an entourage of deacons nearby with walkie talkies. Someone would certainly see me.

The speakers blasted celebratory music overtop the pool, causing ripples to spread in time with the beat. The people in the crowd talked all at once, forming a sound wall preventing my son from moving forward. He was stuck. Tethered to my anxious husband.

I was pissed and determined. You know that mom-itude that results in extra short haircuts and thrift store donations? That was me.

Turning back, I watched my son trying to climb himself up all 6' 5" of Ryan like a cat on a tree. If he could claw his own ears off, too, he would.

It was too dang loud for a baptism!

The pastor was thirty, maybe forty steps away, getting ready to address the masses. This was it. Go. Or go home.

I walked straight toward him, hoping the security team would come in from behind, not ahead. When he noticed my approach, he straightened his shoulders and switched the microphone off.

Don't act crazy, I warned myself. There were probably two men behind me now.

"Hi, Pastor." *Phew!* That took a lot of courage. Now for the wimpy stuff to come out.

"Um. Uh, my son… he's supposed to be baptized." I looked back at David, held securely in Ryan's arms, covering both ears to dampen the sounds. I had to explain.

"It's just… well, he can't…" I felt like crying. This was embarrassing now. Defeated, I let out my breath and spoke plainly.

"It's too loud. Sir." That was as close as I could get to begging.

The pastor followed my gaze and saw the little boy flapping his hands in front of a deeply pained face. He knew that boy. He had seen us at the back of the church.

"What's your name?" he asked. After answering, he nodded and said, "Give me one moment."

The pastor leaned over and instantly one of the security team members was at his ear. With more nodding between them, the man with the walkie talkie was deployed on a mission. A message was relayed to the staff and almost in an instant, the music was turned down to a soft background, the people in the crowd were asked to be silent and stand back. The camera carriers became sparse and the pastor nodded his approval of the orchestrated silencing.

He waved Ryan and David over to the pool.

The pastor made a soft-spoken request over the microphone, "Folks, our first baptism today. Please remain quiet until it is complete."

My heart pounded as Ryan approached and I stepped aside. I pulled my phone out to record the event. Looking back and forth between the screen and reality, I watched my husband wade down the first few steps carrying his son. A minister who was already in the water reached his arms out to receive our boy and cradled him to his chest as they sidled deeper into the water. Ryan had to wait.

It was the most precious sight I have ever laid eyes on. My husband: longing to be with his son. My son: longing to be with a Father.

David prayed with the minister and went silently underneath the water. There was no panic. Only calm. And joy. Onlookers watched in a mixture of curiosity, irritation, and awe.

He was carried back up the steps and handed over to Ryan who now held him close, soaking his clothes in the process.

"My son." He kissed David's forehead. "I'm so proud of you."

We walked out of the pool area with the sound of soft clapping behind us, pats on our shoulders, and thumbs ups from fellow church members. Ryan did not release his son. David was carried and cuddled through the parking lot, chlorine fumes and all.

I schlepped the towel and goody bag behind them mindlessly. My eyes were releasing tears I didn't realize I had held onto for eight long years.

Something good was happening in this family.

Love can, in fact, change people. But the source of the love must be deeper than any human can provide.

Chapter 18

"Forever" Means More Than Adoption

David's baptism offered him a Father who superseded all the male figures he had known on earth. He received love from a Father who was with him in his time of need—one who gave his life meaning and direction. The all-knowing Father would understand David better than anyone could. He could even heal David's hurts, both inside and out.[41] It was more than Ryan or I could ever offer.

That day at the pool, we were all saved by God's grace—each in our own way.[42] Shortly after the adoption was finalized, Ryan also

41 "Praise the Lord, my soul, all my inmost being, praise His holy name. Praise the Lord, my soul, and not all His benefits—He forgive all your sins, and heals all your diseases, who redeems your life from the pit and crowns you with love and compassion, who satisfies your desires with good things, so that your youth is renewed like the eagle's. (Psalm 103:1-5, New International Version)

42 "And we know that in all things God works for the good of those who love him, who have been called according to his purpose. (Romans 8:28, New International Version)

took the plunge and found a new faith. I found courage to tell our story and speak against the fear and doubt that can arise in these situations. David found the family he'd always wanted—one that truly loved him *no matter what.*

Faith, hope, and love redeemed us all.[43] Standing together in family court, we also redefined the meaning of "un-adoptable."

In a later church sermon, the message revolved around answered prayers. In the Bible story the pastor used, a couple named Zechariah and Elizabeth had waited a long time to start a family. By the time a child came along, Zechariah couldn't believe it was even possible, but an Angel from Heaven assured him that it was true: God heard their prayers, they would have a son.[44]

"Mommy," David looked to both Ryan and me sitting together, holding hands. He kept his voice low so he would not disrupt the service.

"Yes, Baby?" I smiled down at him. He was sitting on the ground, holding two action figures in freeze frame.

"That story is just like ours!" He concluded. Even Ryan nodded in agreement.

Then David asked, "How many years did *you* guys pray for a son?"

"Oh, maybe thr—"

---

43 "There are three things that remain—faith, hope, and love—and the greatest of these is love." (1st Corinthians 13:13, The Living Bible)

44 Luke, Chapter 1.

"A *long* time," Ryan interrupted with a glimmer in his eye. I squeezed his hand for a *long* time, too.

"And then God answered your prayer?"

"Yes, Baby," I said. With one more look to Ryan, I added, "He sure did."

My Son.
(March, 2019)

Before we met, if I had known
The reasons why you hadn't grown,
The stories of your mental care,
Or horrors of your dental care,
I might have been a little shocked,
My perception, a bit rocked,
If all at once, I knew of you
I don't know that I would go through
Adopting you,
My son,
My son.

If I heard more about your rage
And acting way below your age,
Insurmountable fears
Which would trigger your tears,
I may have been more cautious
Before I assumed losses.

If all at once, I knew, I knew,
I don't believe that it would do
To keep you,
My son,
My son.

If what we know was then unveiled
And more accurate the forms entailed,
Your deficits in basic skills
And struggles to eat simple meals,
Would scare me far away, away.
I would not be here for you today.

If all at once, I were to learn
My home, my life, would be upturned,
I might have spurned
My son,
My son.

But God had bigger plans, you see,
For you, and now, our family.
Through errors and omissions,
Mysteries and detrition,
We are all together, now, and forever.
We promised that we would never sever

This life we have to support you,
To heal and hold and love on you,
My son,

My son,
I couldn't do it if I knew.

My job is clear for while you're here;
A home of better atmosphere,
A world with three square meals a day,
And mom and dad are here to stay.
A life with us means suffering through
To shed the past that's gripping you.

With God, this is just what we'll do
Because His promises are true,
My son,
My son.
He promises you
Family, love, and future, too.

I see, today, that if I knew
I'd miss out on His promise, too.
For all I'd give, it will return
To me, the mother, in concern.
The patience and truth
Invested in your youth

Will be blessed upon blessed
Because I possessed
The will to accept
Someone called "less than the best,"
And my heart to arrest,
All judgment suppressed,

So it could go through—
The adoption of you,
Just as you are,
My son,
My son.

Afterword

As a family, everyone discovered that with the help of a loving God in their lives, they could do hard things. Even things previously thought to be impossible became possible with His assistance.[45]

The trauma drama, however, did not stop after the adoption day. The family committed thousands upon thousands of hours (and dollars) to remediating his educational delays and addressing his medical concerns to the fullest degree. A special thanks goes out to the occupational therapist, applied behavioral therapist, feeding therapist, physical therapist, hand therapist, vision therapist, art therapist, sensory integration therapist, play therapist, cognitive behavioral therapists, psychiatrist, neurologist, ophthalmologist, attachment specialist, five trauma specialists and seven direct support specialists (we went through a handful), family counselor, five respite providers, countless prayer warriors, a reading specialist, and math tutors. Even though their services were paid for, the family

45 "Jesus looked at them intently and said, 'For humans this is impossible, but for God all things are possible.'" (Matthew 19:26, International Standard Version, Holy Bible)

remains forever indebted to the amazing team of professionals who have come alongside them in this journey. *Thank you for not giving up on our son either.*

Janelle continued homeschooling David for five years. She began a blog titled AdoptionToLife.com (@AdoptionToLife) and has been reaching out to other parents of children from foster care or with special needs. She hopes to continue writing and sharing the voices and dreams of the overlooked and underserved.

Ryan ultimately changed his job and moved the family nearer to extended family to make sure David would grow up with adoring grandparents in his life. He began working with the youth in our local church and has been very active in David's life. He financially backs numerous dance classes and David's passion for musical theatre.

David finally learned to read and now has an insatiable interest in historical accounts and biographies of famous scientists. He plans to go to college for medicine and engineering so he can save lives. He is determined to adopt his own children from foster care and make sure they know how much they are loved. He has authored two children's books awaiting publication, *Adoptive Moms Are Great!* and *Adoptive Dads Are Awesome!* (pending titles). His future is looking bright.

Acknowledgements

To my husband:

Thank you for listening to my thoughts over and over. Your gentleness is a strength I envy. You have been steadfast in your support, a warm light in our home, and a good, good father to our baby.

To my mother, my forever editor:

Thank you for teaching me how to read and write. As you would tell the story, you read so many books to me that I figured out how to read for myself by the age of "free." You made me feel brave enough to tell my story.

To Ryan's father:

Thank you for being the best fly-on-the-wall, unauthorized support for our first week with a child. Thank you for helping us play the famous "farting game" to assist him with healing his body and soul. Thank you for bearing witness to your son's loss of *his* son on the day CPS came to collect him. You were there for him in a way no one else could possibly have been. You will be forever credited with teaching our baby to swim.

Thank you again for reading our love story!

For more on Janelle and David and what they are up to today, please follow the blog, or tune in on social media:

Blog: www.AdoptionToLife.com
Instagram: @AdoptionToLife
Facebook: Facebook.com/AdoptionToLife

If you'd like to reach Janelle Molony to discuss the material or speaking engagements, please reach out at www.JanelleMolony.com/contact

Finally, your honest review is appreciated. Please consider sharing your thoughts with the location of your purchase, on GoodReads.com, with your local support groups, and on social media.

Made in the USA
Las Vegas, NV
19 December 2021

38771256R10114